Knowing

The Faith
of
Anglicans

by

John Rodgers

Anglican House

▶▶

Published as part of of the KNOWING ANGLICANISM series of books by Anglican House, an imprint of Anglican House Publishers, the registered trade name of Anglican House Media Ministry, Inc., Newport Beach, California. Anglican House is a Ministry Partner of the Anglican Church in North America. Contact us at anglicanhousepublishers.org.

Ellen Kirkland, Publisher
Canon Ron Speers, Series Editor

Printed in paperback by Asia Printing Co., Ltd., Seoul, Korea. Printed in newsprint by Thomas Group Printing, New York, NY, USA.

This work is protected under the copyright laws of the United States, Canada, the U.K. and some 90 other countries. No part of this work may be reproduced or transmitted in any form or by any means, including photocopying and recording, or by any information storage and retrieval system, without written permission from the publisher. Any translation of this Work into another language for distribution requires the written permission of the copyright owner, and any such authorized translation is a derivative work in which the copyright owner owns the copyright. All rights are strictly reserved.

All Scripture quotations are from The Holy Bible, English Standard Version® (ESV®), copyright © 2001 by Crossway, a publishing ministry of Good News Publishers. Used with permission. All rights reserved.

© 2021 John H. Rodgers, Jr.
All Rights Strictly Reserved

ISBN 978-1-7359022-8-9 (Paperback Edition)
ISBN 978-1-7376913-0-3 (Bundled Edition)

Dedication

This brief introduction to the 39 Articles of the Anglican Communion is dedicated to the memory of John R. W. Stott and J. I. Packer, biblical theologians par excellence and mentors to us and to generations to come.

Contents

Foreword ix
Preface xi
Introduction xiii

Part One: God and the Apostolic Faith (Articles 1-5)   1

Article 1: Of Faith in the Holy Trinity 3
Article 2: Of the Word or Son of God, which was made very Man 7
Article 3: Of the going down of Christ into Hell 11
Article 4: Of the Resurrection of Christ 14
Article 5: Of the Holy Ghost 18

Part Two: The Rule of Faith (Articles 6-8)   23

Article 6: Of the Sufficiency of the Holy Scriptures for Salvation 25
Article 7: Of the Old Testament 30
Article 8: Of the Three Creeds 34

Part Three: Salvation in Christ (Articles 9-18)   37

Article 9: Of Original or Birth Sin 39
Article 10: Of Free Will 44
Article 11: Of the Justification of Man 47
Article 12: Of Good Works 51
Article 13: Of Works before Justification 54
Article 14: Of Works of Supererogation 57
Article 15: Of Christ alone without Sin 59
Article 16: Of Sin after Baptism 62
Article 17: Of Predestination and Election 65
Article 18: Of obtaining eternal Salvation only by the Name of Christ 69

Part Four: The Church, Sacraments, and the Ordained Ministry (Articles 19-36)   73

Article 19: Of the Church 75
Article 20: Of the Authority of the Church 79
Article 21: Of the Authority of General Councils 83
Article 22: Of Purgatory 86
Article 23: Of Ministering in the Congregation 89
Article 24: Of Speaking in the Congregation in such a Tongue as the people understandeth 92
Article 25: Of the Sacraments 95
Article 26: Of the Unworthiness of the Ministers, which hinders not the effect of the Sacraments 100
Article 27: Of Baptism 104

Article 28: Of the Lord's Supper 108
Article 29: Of the Wicked, which eat not the Body of
   Christ in the use of the Lord's Supper 112
Article 30: Of both Kinds 115
Article 31: Of the one Oblation of Christ finished upon
   the Cross 117
Article 32: Of the Marriage of Priests 120
Article 33: Of excommunicate Persons, how they are to
   be avoided 123
Article 34: Of the Traditions of the Church 127
Article 35: Of the Homilies 131
Article 36: Of Consecration of Bishops and Ministers 134

Part Five: Christianity and Civic Responsibilities (Articles 37-39)   139

Article 37: Of the Power of the Civil Magistrates 141
Article 38: Of Christian Men's Goods, which are
   not common 146
Article 39: Of a Christian Man's Oath 149

Concluding Remarks 153

Foreword

This is a sparkling little book by my long-time friend and mentor, Bishop John Rodgers. When I collaborated with him on his *Zoom Memoirs* last year, I became aware of how comprehensively the Articles of Religion (the "Thirty-nine Articles") had shaped his life and ministry, from his confirmation as a teenager in the Episcopal Church right down to the present. Here he gives a layman's summary of each Article, along with biblical citations and questions for thought and discussion.

This little handbook is a careful condensation of the author's acclaimed 735-page Commentary on the Articles of Religion. Individuals and congregations will find joy and wisdom in the wonderful way the Articles of Religion continue to describe our faith and hope as believers in Christ.

The Thirty-nine Articles of Religion are the only confession of Anglican doctrine recognized historically and globally. Yet they pose certain obstacles to contemporary readers. They are written in Elizabethan prose and some engage particular issues facing the English Reformers in their day. At the same time, the Articles articulate "the faith once for all delivered to the saints." One of the fundamentals of the Articles that define Anglicanism to this day is that nothing can be accepted as doctrine unless it is proven in the Scriptures. So I would encourage readers to search the scripture texts provided alongside each Article since, as our Lord says, "it is they that bear witness about me" (John 5:39).

The Rev. Dr. Stephen Noll
Professor Emeritus, Trinity School for Ministry

Preface

It is a personal pleasure and honor for me to be asked to write this shorter treatment of the 39 Articles. The Articles have played a major role in my life as they were intended to do for all Anglicans, but so seldom do. I pray that this short book will help with the recovery of biblical faithfulness throughout the Anglican world.

Questions have been included for both personal review and reflection and for group discussion in confirmation classes and congregational adult education.

A prayer has been included at the end of each Article, for faith is not only a matter of the mind but of the heart. Also, one or more texts have been included at the end of each Article to remind us that the Articles draw their true authority from being faithful to the Holy Scriptures. Naturally, there are many more texts that could be included, but space does not permit it.

I want to thank the Reverend Dr. Stephen Noll and his wife Peggy for their editorial assistance, for formatting and proof reading. Their assistance has been both a joy and essential.

Introduction

What do Anglicans officially believe? The Churches that separated from the Roman Catholic Church at the time of the great 16th century Reformation had to declare what they stood for, both for the sake of the other Christian Churches and for their own clergy and members. At that point Anglicans set forth the Articles of Religion (originally 42 of them, finally 39), along with the Book of Common Prayer and the Ordinal as the Anglican statement of faith. Canon A5 of the Church of England puts it this way:

> The doctrine of the Church of England is grounded in the holy Scriptures, and in such teachings of the ancient Fathers and Councils of the Church as are agreeable to the said Scriptures. In particular such doctrine is to be found in the Thirty-nine Articles of Religion, the *Book of Common Prayer*(1662) and the Ordinal.

The 39 Articles have been printed at the back of the Book of Common Prayer ever since and are, together with the Apostles Creed and the Athanasian Creed, by far the most widespread of the official statements of Anglican belief. It is difficult to see how one can claim to be an informed Anglican without a familiarity with them, not to mention the godly joy they bring to the reader.

This brief tour of the 39 Articles will focus entirely on the central teaching of each Article and will suggest some ways the

Article applies to our life in Christ, both as individual believers and as congregations, whether Anglican or not.

There is a richness in the Articles that will not be examined here; for a fuller appreciation of their teaching the reader is directed to *Essential Truths for Christians: A Commentary on the Anglican Thirty-Nine Articles and an Introduction to Systematic Theology* by the same author, also reprinted as *The Thirty-nine Articles*.

The 39 Articles can be divided into five parts: Part One, God and the Apostolic Faith; Part Two, The Rule of Faith; Part Three, Salvation in Christ; Part Four, The Church, Sacraments, and the Ordained Ministry; and Part Five, Christianity and Civic Responsibilities.

Part One

God and the Apostolic Faith (Articles 1-5)

These five Articles are so essential to the Christian Faith that even at the Reformation there was no disagreement about their content. Today, however, in a more skeptical period in Western society, there are many outside and inside the Churches who would not agree with much in these Articles. We need to consider them and the truth they assert most carefully.

Article 1

Of Faith in the Holy Trinity

> There is but one living and true God, everlasting, without body, parts, or passions; of infinite power, wisdom, and goodness; the Maker, and Preserver of all things both visible and invisible. And in unity of this Godhead there be three Persons of one substance, power, and eternity; the Father, the Son, and the Holy Ghost.

This Article treats two great truths: 1. the magnificence of God; and 2. the Triune nature of God's Being. We will take them in order.

The Magnificence of God.

It is instructive that the Articles begin with God and not with the Bible. Why? If God is not Who he is, it really is not worth our effort in thinking through how we come to know Him.

Also, Christian doctrines are so interconnected and interdependent that no matter where we start, we must assume a great deal to be discussed later. There are other reasons why we should start with God: there was no controversy over the greatness of God at the time the Articles were formulated; it is always good to start on common ground.

Even today, in our skeptical culture, if you ask an atheist what "God" he is denying, the chances are it will be God as He is set forth in this Article. Lastly, since God is the center and key to everything, it is right and good to begin with Him. First things first.

What is God like and what are His characteristics or "attributes," as theology usually refers to them? The Article confesses that God is One, there is none like Him and none alongside of Him. He alone is the only living and true God. "*Shema, shema* [Hear, hear], O Israel, the Lord our God is One" is the central Creed of Israel and the Old Testament. He is unlike idols of wood or clay or stone that are neither alive nor truly God. He alone is to be in the center of our hearts and lives.

And what is the One and true living God like? He alone is eternal, having neither a beginning nor an end, unlike all that He has created. That means He is always there to help us and to correct us if need be. It is His nature ever to be beyond our understanding, and this truth marks His difference from the creation which He has made and preserves in being. He does not change. He does not grow old or out of date. He is always what His characteristics declare Him to be: righteous, caring, merciful, loving, all knowing, wise, omnipresent, and omnipotent. He is pure Spirit, having no body and no parts.

This Article speaks of God's "passions" in a particular manner, drawn from philosophy of the day. It meant that God cannot be limited or frustrated by powers other than Himself. There is no one or no thing on His level of Being. We could say it is an aspect of His sovereignty. We use the word "passion" differently today to refer to our desires and feelings, both of which God has aplenty, as any reading of the Bible makes clear.

His glory is the magnificence of all His attributes taken together and shining forth so full and dazzling that we can only fall down and worship before Him. This is why the Westminster Shorter Catechism states that "man's chief end is to glorify God and enjoy Him forever."

Here we learn that His greatness is such that He is more than able to meet all our needs and rescue us from all difficulties, even from His own righteous judgment. He alone is worthy of our devotion, which is His due.

The Triune Nature of God

Having made clear both the character of the One, true and living God and His attributes, the Article directs us to His threefold (or Triune) Being, to the doctrine of the Trinity. Stated simply, God is one Being and within Himself there are three Persons, or interrelated centers of self-awareness and activity. This is mysterious and beyond our comprehension, but the biblical revelation is unequivocal: God is God the Father, God the Son and God the Holy Spirit. Numerous texts of Scripture make it clear that all three Persons participate in His relationships with us and in all His acts in time and space. The Risen Jesus commands His Church to baptize "in the name of the Father and of the Son and of the Holy Spirit" (Matt 28:19). So also St. Paul concludes a letter: "the grace of the Lord Jesus Christ, and the love of God and the fellowship of the Holy Spirit be with you" (2 Cor 13:14).

Greatly significant is the fact that all three Persons cooperate in our salvation. Were we to deny the full divinity of the Person and work of any of the Persons of the Trinity, we would deny our salvation; for the Father sent the Son, the Son took our place and the Spirit opens our hearts to receive the grace given us in the Son, to the glory of God the Father.

When all is said and done, we celebrate the threefold nature of God because it is true, not because we fully understand its mystery.

Prayer

Almighty and everlasting God, you have given to us your servants grace, by the confession of a true faith, to acknowledge the glory of the eternal Trinity, and in the power of your divine Majesty to worship the unity: Keep us steadfast in this faith and worship, and bring us at last to see you in your one and eternal glory, O Father; who with the Son and the Holy Spirit live and reign, one God, for ever and ever. *Amen.*

Scripture Texts

2 Samuel 7:22 "Therefore you are great, O Lord God. For there is none like you, and there is no God beside you, according to all that we have heard with our ears."

Galatians 4:6 "And because you are sons, God has sent the Spirit of his Son into our hearts, crying, 'Abba! Father!'"

Questions for Discussion

1. Which of the attributes of God do you most often consciously call to mind?
2. Why is God worthy of our ultimate dependence and worship?
3. Which Person of the Trinity do you think of first? Why?
4. What are the idols of our culture that people put in the place of God in their hearts?

Article 2

Of the Word or Son of God, which was made very Man

The Son, which is the Word of the Father, begotten from everlasting of the Father, the very and eternal God, and of one substance with the Father, took Man's nature in the womb of the blessed Virgin, of her substance: so that two whole and perfect Natures, that is to say, the Godhead and Manhood, were joined together in one Person, never to be divided, whereof is one Christ, very God, and very Man; who truly suffered, was crucified, dead, and buried, to reconcile his Father to us, and to be a sacrifice, not only for original guilt, but also for actual sins of men.

At the heart of the Christian Faith is Christ Himself. It is often said "Christianity is Christ." The early Church adopted as its motto the Greek word *IXTHYS* ("fish") meaning, "Jesus Christ, the Son of God and Savior." This refers both to His Person as Son of God and to His saving Work on the Cross. It is essential that we understand Who He is, for His death on the Cross makes no biblical sense unless you understand who it is that is dying and why.

This Article has two assertions of basic Christian belief: 1. the Incarnation of God the Son; and 2. Christ's work of atonement on the Cross.

The Incarnation

First, we consider the Incarnation ("in-flesh") of God the Son, the Word of the Father. He is more than a founding teacher such as is found in the world's religions. He is truly ("very") God, God the Son. He is the eternal God, as described in some detail in Article 1. He is, in the words of the Nicene Creed, "of one substance with the Father." This leads to such remarkable statements as: "He who has seen me has seen the Father" and "The Father and I are One" or "Before Abraham was, I AM" (the name of God). He is God's self-expression as The Word. The Prophets came with *a word* from God – "Thus saith the Lord" – but Jesus is *the Word of God* in person. In and through the apostolic Scriptures we can literally see God in the flesh in our time and space.

Jesus is not only divine in the fullest sense, but He is also truly ("very") Man as well. As God created Man in His image, male and female, so He has sent His Son, the second Adam, Who is the "image of the invisible God" (Col. 1:15). He has all our human characteristics, sin excepted. When we see Him in and through the Scriptures and by the various means of grace, we see what we are created to be and into Whose image we are being transformed (2 Cor 3:18).

Just as Jesus is utterly unique, He was conceived uniquely, being born of the Holy Spirit and the Virgin Mary. By taking human nature into His divine Person, He became one Person in two natures, which is unique to Him. "In Him all the fulness of the Godhead dwelt bodily" (Col 2:9). And His two natures are never to be divided, that is, His Being as one Person in two natures is eternal, so profound and abiding is God's love for us. The Incarnation is mysterious and incomprehensible to us, but it is clear in Holy Scripture and essential to God's saving work for us.

The Atonement

Second, the Article speaks of Jesus' atoning work upon the Cross. Why did Jesus assume our nature? Why did He become incarnate of the Virgin Mary? He did this because He came to die *for us*. This was shocking news to God's people, including the Apostles at first, for no one thought that the promised Messiah would suffer and die. But Jesus Christ did just that!

It is important to be clear that Jesus really did suffer and die on the Cross. This was denied by the Gnostics in the early days of the Church and is denied by Muslims to this day. But why did He come so to suffer and died for us? What did the Cross accomplish?

The simple answer stated in the Nicene Creed is that He died "for us and our salvation." There are four main ways that the New Testament writers view the accomplishments of the Cross.

This Article highlights what is perhaps the main one: He came to be both our representative and our substitute. The punishment He bore on the Cross was our punishment, our due because of our sin. The perfect righteousness that He lived and the sinlessness of His sacrifice for us, He did that it might be reckoned by God to our account, which we receive by faith. In one astonishing act, God both propitiated (appeased) His own wrath as the righteous judge of us as sinners and expiated (covered) our sin, so He would see it no more. On the Cross Christ brought about the Father's reconciliation with us and our reconciliation with God. Only the one who is both God and man could accomplish this, for only God's "death" could count for all humanity. And, God cannot die in His divine nature, nor is there another man than Jesus who can be our sinless representative and sacrificial substitute. As Paul put it: "Oh, the depth of the riches and wisdom and knowledge of God!" (Rom 11:33)

Prayer

Almighty God, you have poured upon us the new light of your incarnate Word: Grant that this light, kindled in our hearts, may shine forth in our lives; through Jesus Christ our Lord, who lives and reigns with you in the unity of the Holy Spirit, one God, now and forever. *Amen.*

Scripture Texts

John 1:1,14 "In the beginning was the Word, and the Word was with God and the Word was God. . . . And the Word became flesh and dwelt among us, and we have seen His glory, glory as of the only Son from the Father, full of grace and truth."

Romans 3:23-25 "For all have sinned and fall short of the glory of God, and are justified by His grace as a gift, through the redemption that is in Christ Jesus, whom God put forward as a propitiation by His blood, to be received by faith. This was to show God's righteousness, because in his divine forbearance he passed over former sins."

Questions for Discussion

1. Why is it essential that Jesus be fully God and fully Man?
2. How does the Incarnation differ from Jesus being a man filled with the Holy Spirit?
3. What is the difference between Jesus just being our representative and His being our representative and substitute?

Article 3

Of the going down of Christ into Hell

As Christ died for us, and was buried, so also is it to be believed, that he went down into Hell.

This Article makes one point about a rather obscure doctrine, Christ's descent into hell. This doctrine came late into universal Christian acceptance. While it had circulated earlier, it was added to the Athanasian Creed in the 5th century and to the Apostle's Creed in the 8th century. It has lately been modified in recent Prayer Books to replace "hell" with "the dead."

There are a variety of interpretations of this doctrine, based on the two biblical texts from the First Letter of Peter (see below).

The text from 1 Peter 3 suggests that Christ went into Sheol (the Old Testament place of the dead) to announce final condemnation to the unsaved who have spurned God's word from Noah's time on (cf. 1 Cor 1:18).

The text from 1 Peter 4 suggests that Christ went to preach the Gospel to those in Sheol who had not heard the Gospel and had died unconverted, in order that they might repent and believe and come alive in the Spirit. This would not be a second chance to believe, for the Bible clearly teaches that there is not a second chance after death for those who die rejecting the Gospel. It would be a first chance to respond to the Gospel for many, since many died before the Gospel was preached or had lived and died never hearing the Gospel, because no one had come to that part of the world to preach the Gospel to them.

Both interpretations understand "hell" not to refer to the final place of torment but rather to the place where the dead go

Part One: God and the Apostolic Faith

who are not in Christ and who await the final judgment at Jesus' Second Coming. Christians at death go directly to Paradise in the presence of Jesus.

Both interpretations hold the common belief that Jesus underwent the full experience of death, which was essential since He is our representative and substitute before God. We never have to go where our Savior has not gone before.

Prayer

O God of the living, on this day your Son our Savior descended to the place of the dead: Look with kindness on all of us who wait in hope for liberation from the corruption of sin and death and give us a share in the glory of the children of God; through Jesus Christ your Son our Lord. *Amen.*

Scripture Texts

1 Peter 3:18-20 "For Christ also suffered once for sins, the righteous for the unrighteous, that he might bring us to God, being put to death in the flesh but made alive in the spirit, in which [in Jesus' spirit, while His body lay in the tomb] He went and proclaimed to the spirits in prison, because they formerly did not obey when God's patience waited in the days of Noah, while the ark was being prepared."

1 Peter 4:6 "For this is why the gospel was preached even to those who are dead, that though judged in the flesh the way people are, they might live in the spirit the way God does."

Questions for discussion

1. Do you think it is better to replace "hell" with "the dead" in the Creed? Why?
2. What comfort does it give you to know that Jesus suffered death fully and completely?
3. How do you interpret these two difficult verses? What interpretation seems most likely to you?

Article 4

Of the Resurrection of Christ

Christ did truly rise again from death, and took again his body, with flesh, bones, and all things appertaining to the perfection of Man's nature; wherewith he ascended into Heaven, and there sitteth, until he returns to judge all Men at the last day.

This Article directs us to the heart of the Gospel when taken together with the work of Christ on the Cross (Article 2). It addresses three main themes of Christ's Work: 1. the Resurrection of Christ; 2. the Ascension of Christ; and 3. the Second Coming of Christ for final judgment of all mankind.

The Resurrection

The Kenyan liturgy states: "We set our hope on the Risen Christ." The Risen Christ as presented in Scripture is set forth as possessing all our spiritual and bodily characteristics. His Resurrection is not the same as the examples of resuscitation that we find in the Bible, such as that of Lazarus or the son of the widow of Nain or the centurion's daughter. They were brought back to live life in this world as they did before they died, and they did die later. Christ was not resuscitated back into His pre-Resurrection life; He rose victorious over death and would die no more; death has no dominion over Him. Just the opposite, death itself was vanquished by Him and will in the last day be removed from reality altogether.

We cannot say that He was raised spiritually but not bodily. The historical evidence for the miracle of Christ's bodily Resurrection is overwhelming. Many who have started out to debunk it have ended up affirming it, even writing books about it. His appearances to the disciples in which He was touchable and ate with them, the change in the Apostles from hiding fearfully to being bold witnesses to His Resurrection, their willingness to die for their faith, the Empty Tomb, the earliest witness by the women while the men were still hiding, the inability of the opposition to present the body, the rise and growth of the Church while eyewitnesses to His death and Resurrection were still alive and available, and the remarkable conversion of Paul are just a few evidences of His Resurrection.

The Resurrection of Christ prefigures and anticipates the resurrection of all who belong to Him through the Gospel and in faith. In the end we too shall share in this Resurrection glory, of which He is the first-fruit and forerunner. In fact, we have the beginning of our resurrection now in the indwelling of the Holy Spirit in us.

The Resurrection not only anticipates our resurrection in Christ, it sets the seal of truth on all of Jesus' previous life and teaching. It was the light of the Resurrection, for example, that opened the eyes of the disciples to see that the Cross was not a defeat but the great act of God's redemption and the seal of God's approval on the work of the Son. Christ defeated sin, death and the Devil on the Cross and in the Resurrection. He did this all on our behalf and for our benefit now and in the days to come.

The Ascension

After a forty-day period of instruction of His disciples, our Risen Lord ascended to sit enthroned at the right hand of God the Father, the seat of cosmic authority. He explained to His disciples just before He ascended: "All authority in heaven and on earth has been given unto me." From this throne He exercises His authority in and through the events of history, and through the actions of His faithful followers. This throne is also the sanctuary in which "He ever lives to make intercession for us" (Heb 7:25). Because of Christ's heavenly reign, St. Paul can say "All things work together for good to those who love God and are called according to His purpose" (Rom 8:28).

The Final Judgment

Lastly, this Article speaks of the Risen Christ's Second Coming in glory to judge the living and the dead, i.e., those who have died and those still alive at His Coming. As the Scriptures clearly teach, all of us must in the end give an account for the life we have lived. For any who have refused the Gospel or the knowledge that was theirs through creation and conscience, it will be a judgment that will lead to final condemnation. For believers whose names are written in the Lamb's Book of Life, "there is now no condemnation to those who are in Christ Jesus." There will be a judgment on our works (Rev 20:12) and an entrance into glory. Because of this we look forward to His return and cry, "Maranatha! Come Lord Jesus!"

Prayer

Almighty God, who through your only begotten Son Jesus Christ overcame death and opened to us the gate of everlasting life: Grant that we, who celebrate with joy the day of the Lord's resurrection, may, by your life-giving Spirit, be delivered from sin and raised from death: through Jesus Christ our Lord, who lives and reigns with you and the Holy Spirit, one God, now and forever. *Amen*

Scripture Texts

1 Peter 1: 3 "Blessed be the God and Father of our Lord Jesus Christ! According to his great mercy, he has caused us to be born again to a living hope through the resurrection of Jesus Christ from the dead."

Hebrews 10:12 "But when Christ had offered for all time a single sacrifice for sins, he sat down at the right hand of God."

2 Corinthians 5:10 "For we must all appear before the judgment seat of Christ, so that each one may receive what is due for what he has done in the body, whether good or evil."

Questions for Discussion

1. Why is it wrong to say that Jesus rose spiritually and not bodily? What difference does it make?
2. If "the prayers of a righteous man avail much," what does the intercession of Christ for you mean?
3. Why do we all have to be judged in the final judgment?
4. If Christ is to be our Judge, how is it possible that we can look forward to His return with joy and gladness?

Article 5

Of the Holy Ghost

The Holy Ghost, proceeding from the Father and the Son, is of one substance, majesty, and glory, with the Father and the Son, very and eternal God.

This Article does two things. It declares 1. that the Holy Spirit is fully God; and 2. that He proceeds from both the Father and the Son.

The Person of the Holy Spirit

Having dealt with the doctrine of the Trinity in Article 1, this Article simply underlines the full divinity and Personhood of the Holy Spirit (Holy Ghost). The Holy Spirit is in every way fully God and part of the Godhead.

The Spirit Proceeding from the Father and the Son

The Article points out that the Spirit proceeds from both the Father and the Son. To "proceed" from the Father and Son means that the Father and the Son possess logical but not chronological priority to the Spirit, as in "light from light." This Article puts Anglicans in agreement with St. Augustine and the Church in the West, stating that the Spirit is the mutual bond of love of the Father and the Son. The Church in the East has never accepted the "dual procession" of the Spirit from both the Father and the Son. The Orthodox hold that the Spirit proceeds only from the

Father. While this may seem a trivial matter to many, it remains a block to further ecumenical agreement in the wider Church.

The Holy Spirit has at times been referred to as an attribute of the Godhead, or as a life-force, an "It," due to the fact that so little preaching and teaching has been done concerning the Holy Spirit. He has also been referred to as the shy member of the Trinity for His focus is on the Son and not on Himself. Some Pentecostal churches, on the other hand, treat Him as an independent agent not essentially united to the Father and the Son. Many contemporary Anglicans, due to the recent charismatic movement, have recovered a balance in understanding the Spirit and His work.

At the Last Supper, Jesus promised: "I will ask the Father, and he will give you another Paraclete, to be with you forever" (John 14:16). In using the word "another" ("of the same kind") and "Paraclete" (translated "Counselor," "Advocate" or "Helper"), Jesus makes clear that this Person has the same Being as the Father and the Son. Our Counselor is God the Holy Spirit with us and nothing less.

The Work of the Spirit

Since no other Article deals with the Holy Spirit directly, it seems right to mention some of what the Holy Spirit does regarding our relation to God, to our fellow Christians, to non-Christians and to the world in general.

Since the Holy Spirit is fully God, He has been involved with creation from the beginning and active throughout human history (cf. Gen 1:2). From the first Pentecost on, He has been at work with God's people in an expanded and deepened way. John the Baptist told us that when the Messiah came, He would baptize us with the Holy Spirit. The Apostle Paul tells us that in Christ we are all made participants in the indwelling of the Holy

Spirit (Rom 5:5). He exhorts us that both individually and as congregations we should continually seek to be filled with the Holy Spirit.

What does the indwelling Holy Spirit do in and through us? A few things stand out in Scripture and in our experience. He is the one who opens our hearts to receive the Gospel. He is the renewing and sanctifying Spirit, helping us grow more and more like Christ. He produces in us the fruits of love, joy, peace, patience, kindness, goodness, faithfulness, gentleness and self-control (Gal 5:22-23). He helps us resist external temptation and inward inclinations to sin, that is, He helps us grow and become more and more like Christ. He is the bond of unity between all Christians, as He is the bond of love between the Father and the Son in the Godhead. He guides us, making Scripture or the words of a familiar hymn come alive and speak to us, or by nudging us to do a good work, or convicting our conscience so that we are led to repentance. The Spirit sovereignly gives and distributes the charismatic gifts to us for the upbuilding of the body of Christ, the Church (1 Cor 12:1-13). On occasion, He works miracles through us, as He did among the first Apostles.

Finally, His presence in and with us is the guarantee of our final glory to come in the new heaven and earth, so He is called a "down-payment" or "the first installment of the glory that is to come," thus He is the author of our sure and certain hope.

In short, by the grace of God, the Spirit is God with us and intimately within us, an inexpressible gift and the source of our humble, thankful, joy.

Prayer

O God, who on this day taught the hearts of your faithful people by sending them the light of your Holy Spirit: Grant us by the same Spirit to have a right judgment in all things, and evermore to rejoice in his holy comfort; through Jesus Christ your Son our Lord, who lives and reigns with you, in the unity if the Holy Spirit, one God, for ever and ever. *Amen.*

Scripture Texts

John 15:26 "But when the Helper [Paraclete] comes, whom I will send to you from the Father, the Spirit of truth, who proceeds from the Father, he will bear witness about me."

2 Corinthians 13:14 "The grace of the Lord Jesus Christ and the love of God and the fellowship of the Holy Spirit be with you all."

Questions for Discussion

1. In your experience, has the Holy Spirit been neglected or over-emphasized in the preaching and teaching of the Church?
2. Why is it wrong to refer to the Holy Spirit as "it"?
3. Of the works of the Spirit listed, which of His activities have you experienced?
4. How do we seek to keep on being filled with the Holy Spirit?

Part Two

The Rule of Faith (Articles 6-8)

Anglicans are biblical Christians and creedal Christians. When we are considering the truth of theological statements of belief, we must have a "canon," a standard or measuring rod of truth. For Anglicans, the Bible is the supreme standard of truth, which is summed up in the Creeds. This section sets forth the "rule of faith" that Anglicans use in this regard.

Article 6

Of the Sufficiency of the Holy Scriptures for Salvation

Holy Scripture containeth all things necessary to salvation: so that whatsoever is not read therein, nor may be proved thereby, is not to be required of any man, that it should be believed as an Article of the Faith, or be thought requisite or necessary to salvation. In the name of the Holy Scripture we do understand those canonical Books of the Old and New Testament, of whose authority was never any doubt in the Church.

Of the Names and Number of the Canonical Books.

Genesis, The First Book of Samuel, The Book of Esther, Exodus, The Second Book of Samuel, The Book of Job, Leviticus, The First Book of Kings, The Psalms, Numbers, The Second Book of Kings, The Proverbs, Deuteronomy, The First Book of Chronicles, Ecclesiastes or Preacher, Joshua, The Second Book of Chronicles, Cantica, or Songs of Solomon, Judges, The First Book of Esdras, Four Prophets the greater, Ruth, The Second Book of Esdras, Twelve Prophets the less.

And the other Books (as Hierome saith) the Church doth read for example of life and instruction of manners; but yet doth it not apply them to establish any doctrine; such are these following:

The Third Book of Esdras, The rest of the Book of Esther, The Fourth Book of Esdras, The Book of Wisdom,

> The Book of Tobias, Jesus the Son of Sirach, The Book of Judith, Baruch the Prophet, The Song of the Three Children, The Prayer of Manasses, The Story of Susanna, The First Book of Maccabees, Of Bel and the Dragon, The Second Book of Maccabees.
>
> All the Books of the New Testament, as they are commonly received, we do receive, and account them Canonical.

This Article establishes one of the pillars of the Anglican and Reformation faith, *sola scriptura* (Scripture alone), which means we teach what is in Scripture and that we test our teaching supremely by what is in Scripture.

This Article treats three matters: 1. the sufficiency of Scripture for salvation; 2. the consequences of that sufficiency; and 3. the list of the biblical books that are authoritative in the Church as the Word of God written.

The Sufficiency of Scripture

Personal salvation depends on faith in Jesus Christ as Lord and Savior, and this faith comes to us "through the revelation of Christ according to the Scriptures." This Article declares that such knowledge is found in full sufficiency in the Bible as God's Word written. "Sufficiency" means all that is needed for a purpose, not all that is possible. A road map, not a world atlas, is sufficient to get you from point A to point B, in this case, from sin to salvation. Everything necessary to such knowledge is found there. There is no need to search the world's religions, or to read the latest popular theological book to come to saving faith in Jesus Christ as your Lord and Savior. Just ponder seriously the Holy Scriptures and especially the New Testament.

The Consequences of Sufficiency

Given the sufficiency of Scripture for salvation, there is no need nor any authorization for adding anything to what is set forth in Scripture as necessary for salvation. The Roman Catholic Church, for example, has often insisted on one's affirmation of the doctrine of purgatory or of transubstantiation or of the infallibility of the Pope before being accepted for baptism. Certain sects, e.g., the Mormons, have added their special books as part of the Scripture, leading them to require submission to different doctrines concerning the Person and work of Christ as necessary to salvation. Anglicans hold that no additions of doctrine not found in nor deduced from Scripture must be required for salvation in Christ.

The Canonical Books

At the time of the Reformation there were two main versions of the Bible, one including books that were initially not found in the Old Testament of Jesus' time and one including books written later in Greek and then incorporated into the Old Testament. At the Reformation, Anglicans agreed with the other Reforming Churches to restrict the canon (list of biblical books to be read as authoritative in the life of the Church) to the Hebrew Old Testament and those New Testament books written by one of the Apostles or under their authority. In short, what we find in our usual Bibles today are covered in the list of this Article. The names listed here are a bit different, but the actual content is the same.

One thing unique to Anglicans is that we sometimes bind, in a separate section of our Bibles, the writings of those books of the Greek Old Testament which are referred to as the Apocrypha. We do not consider these books inspired or authoritative for doctrine but as providing historical information helpful to interpreting the Scriptures and giving examples of godly living. In the Roman Catholic and Eastern Orthodox Churches, these writings are part of the canon and are held to be inspired and authoritative. This is not so in Anglicanism, for they contain some teachings contrary to the teaching of the New Testament, and they have never been accepted universally by Jews or Christians.

Prayer

Blessed Lord who caused all Holy Scriptures to be written for our learning: Grant us so to hear them, read, mark, learn, and inwardly digest them, that by patience and the comfort of your holy Word we may embrace and ever hold fast the blessed hope of everlasting life, which you have given us in our Savior Jesus Christ, who lives and reigns with you and the Holy Spirit, one God, for ever and ever. *Amen.*

Scripture Texts

Matthew 22:29 "But Jesus answered them, 'You are wrong because you know neither the Scriptures nor the power of God.'"

2 Timothy 3:16-17 "All Scripture is breathed out by God and profitable for teaching, for reproof, for correction, and for training in righteousness, that the man of God may be competent, equipped for every good work."

Questions for Discussion

1. How would you answer a person who asked you, "What must I know to become a Christian?"
2. Can you mention any books that one of the cults has added to the Scriptures?
3. How would you go about using the Bible as a standard to consider the truthfulness of a world religion or someone's religious opinions?

Article 7

Of the Old Testament

The Old Testament is not contrary to the New: for both in the Old and New Testament everlasting life is offered to Mankind by Christ, who is the only Mediator between God and Man, being both God and Man. Wherefore they are not to be heard, which feign that the old Fathers did look only for transitory promises. Although the Law given from God by Moses, as touching Ceremonies and Rites, do not bind Christian men, nor the Civil precepts thereof ought of necessity to be received in any commonwealth; yet notwithstanding, no Christian man whatsoever is free from the obedience of the Commandments which are called Moral.

This Article has two main points: 1. the continuity of the Old and New Testaments in Christ; and 2. the abiding authority of its moral instruction.

The Continuity of Old and New Testaments

This Article begins with a negative because from the days of the early Church down to today some Christians diminish the status and authority of the Old Testament and locate all authority in the New Testament. One hears people saying things like: "I love Jesus, so full of grace and love, but I will have nothing to do with the God of the Old Testament, so vengeful and legalistic."

This attitude misconstrues both Jesus and the Old Testament, which was Jesus' Bible. Jesus said: "Do not think I have come to abolish the Law or the Prophets; I have not come to abolish them but to fulfill them" (Matt 5:17). He actually deepens our call to obey God and follow Him. A careful reading of the Old Testament will find a great deal of God's love as well as His righteous judgment. And a careful reading of the New Testament will disclose a great deal of accountability and God's judgment as well as grace and love taught there. In both Testaments we find the continuity of God loving and disciplining His people. We find this continuity fully expressed in God's various covenants from Abraham to Noah to Moses to David and culminating in the New Covenant or Testament in Jesus, instituted at the Last Supper, Good Friday and Easter Sunday.

At the center of both Testaments is God's Word, Who became incarnate in Jesus Christ, Who fulfilled the expectations of the Messiah as found in the Old Testament and Who offers us Salvation as we put our faith in God's Word and follow Him.

The Authority of the Moral Commandments

God's revelation of Himself unfolds in progressive stages, like acts in a great drama. Down through history, He reveals more of Himself and deepens our responsibility to follow Him. This means that some of the things His people were called to do before the coming of Christ no longer apply, since Christ has fulfilled their intention (cf. the Epistle to the Hebrews). Our understanding of any part of the Scripture must be understood by God's fullest revelation of Himself in Christ. As the Risen Jesus Himself did when "beginning with Moses and all the Prophets, he interpreted to them in all the Scriptures the things concerning Himself" (Luke 24:27).

This development of revelation applies to God's commandments as well. The civil laws were written for Israel as a nation among the nations of the world, but the Church is not a nation of that sort. So, they are not binding on the Church. Of course, all nations would do well to consider the Bible's civil commands, which are in many aspects full of abiding wisdom.

The ceremonial rules and regulations of the Old Testament have all been fulfilled in Christ, so they too are no longer binding on the Church. For example, Passover is fulfilled in the Lord's Supper. Messianic believers and all Christians may freely and wisely choose to continue keeping such feasts and ceremonies as they wish, for they all reflect Jesus, but they are not binding.

The main statement of biblical morality, which the Prayer Book includes in its Catechism, is the Ten Commandments (Exod 20:1-17). These commandments are expressions of God's own nature and the moral order in which He created us. In Christ they are not only binding, but they are also deepened. He reveals that obedience to the moral law includes the inclination of our hearts, as well as our thoughts and actions, as Jesus makes clear in the Sermon on the Mount. If we covet, we are guilty of idolatry. If we lust, we are guilty of fornication and idolatry. This is true even if we take no action along those lines. Supremely, if we fail to love God with all our heart, soul, mind, and strength and our neighbor as ourselves, we are guilty before God.

How thankful we must be that there is grace for the sinner in Christ! And how wise are His paths set forth in the commandments.

Prayer

O God, the strength of all who put their trust in you: Mercifully accept our prayers, and because through the weakness of our mortal nature, we can do no good thing without you, grant us the help of your grace, that in keeping your commandments we may please you both in will and deed; through Jesus Christ our Lord, who lives and reigns with you and the Holy Spirit, one God, forever and ever. *Amen.*

Scripture Texts

Psalm 19:8 "The precepts of the Lord are right, rejoicing the heart; the commandment of the Lord is pure, enlightening the eyes."

Matthew 5:20 "For I tell you, unless your righteousness exceeds that of the scribes and Pharisees, you will never enter the kingdom of heaven."

John 5:39-40 "You search the Scriptures because you think that in them you have eternal life: and it is they that bear witness about me, yet you refuse to come to me that you may have life."

Questions for Discussion

1. What in the Old Testament has troubled you? How did you deal with that?
2. Have you ever attended a Passover service on Maundy Thursday? In what way is the Lord's Supper a fulfillment of the Passover?
3. If we are not saved by our good works, in what way are the moral commandments of the Bible binding on us as Christians?

Article 8

Of the Three Creeds

The Three Creeds, Nicene Creed, Athanasius's Creed, and that which is commonly called the Apostles' Creed, ought thoroughly to be received and believed: for they may be proved by most certain warrants of Holy Scripture.

Anglicans affirm and use all three of these Ecumenical or Catholic creeds in worship and instruction. The reason they do so is because they summarize what is found in Scripture. The authority of the Creeds lies in their accordance with Scripture.

All three Creeds are Trinitarian, naming the Father, the Son, and the Holy Spirit. The Apostles' Creed is the simplest and is used in Morning and Evening Prayer. The Nicene Creed emphasizes that Jesus is fully God and Man and is used in the Holy Communion service. The Athanasian Creed is less often used liturgically but reminds the Church that confession of the full catholic and apostolic faith is necessary for salvation.

Historically, the Creeds grew in length as clauses were added to refute encroaching errors in the Church's teaching. These historic heresies keep reappearing in modern form, so the Creeds serve as a protection for the Church, warning us not to go down wrong theological paths.

Anglican Churches are in continuity with the ancient Church. It is said by some that we Anglicans believe in one God, two Testaments, the three Creeds and four Councils of the first five centuries. Anglicans have always made it their boast that we are not seeking to present some new, novel theology or to be in any way idiosyncratic, but rather to affirm and live in and by the historic faith of the Church as grounded in the Old and New Testaments and passed on to us through the generations.

Prayer

Let your continual mercy, O Lord, cleanse and defend your Church; and, because it cannot continue in safety without your help, protect and govern it always by your goodness; through Jesus Christ our Lord, who lives and reigns with you and the Holy Spirit, one God, now and forever. *Amen.*

Scripture Text

2 Timothy 1:13 "Follow the pattern of the sound words that you have heard from me, in the faith and love that are in Christ Jesus."

Questions for Discussion

1. Take the Apostles' Creed and see if you can find a biblical text that supports each clause.
2. Which of the creeds do you know best? Why?
3. Can you think of a modern heresy that is refuted by the creeds?

Part Three

Salvation in Christ (Articles 9-18)

"The saying is trustworthy and deserving of full acceptance, that Christ Jesus came into the world to save sinners" (1 Timothy 1:15). This "comfortable word," as the Prayer Book puts it, is at the heart of the central section of the Articles. It is also at the heart of the Reformers' recovery of the biblical Gospel, summarized in the *"sola*'s" (Latin for "only"). We are saved "only by Christ," "only by grace," and "only by faith," because Jesus has done it all in His life, death, and Resurrection for us as our substitute.

These Reformation doctrines are intricately and necessarily connected. Man's utter bondage in "original sin" calls forth God's judgment and wrath but also calls forth His sovereign act of mercy in sending His sinless Son to take upon Himself the sins of the world "for us." This act alone leads to the "justification" of man by grace through faith alone, apart from any "works" done before, during, or after conversion (Eph. 2:8). By receiving God's grace as a gift, the believer is born again and enabled by the Holy Spirit to produce the fruit of love.

This entire act of salvation is according to God's eternal purpose, whereby He elects those who will be saved and assures them of the promise of eternal life in Christ, as proclaimed by Peter shortly after Pentecost: "there is no other name under heaven given among men by which we must be saved" (Acts 4:12).

In this section we will read of why we need salvation and how we are saved in Christ. We find ourselves at the heart of the Gospel and in some serious conflict with teachings that divided Protestants and Catholics at the Reformation. Because of these conflicts, this section is longer than the previous sections.

Article 9

Of Original or Birth Sin

Original sin standeth not in the following of Adam, (as the Pelagians do vainly talk;) but it is the fault and corruption of the Nature of every man, that naturally is engendered of the offspring of Adam; whereby man is very far gone from original righteousness, and is of his own nature inclined to evil, so that the flesh lusteth always contrary to the Spirit; and therefore in every person born into this world, it deserveth God's wrath and damnation. And this infection of nature doth remain, yea in them that are regenerated; whereby the lust of the flesh, called in Greek, φρονημα σαρκος, (which some do expound the wisdom, some sensuality, some the affection, some the desire, of the flesh), is not subject to the Law of God. And although there is no condemnation for them that believe and are baptized; yet the Apostle doth confess, that concupiscence and lust hath of itself the nature of sin.

The doctrine of original sin is found in Scripture and has been embraced by the Church's Ecumenical Councils. At the same time, the doctrine is mysterious and leads us into difficulties which we are not entirely able to reconcile in our minds, although in our experience we find it describes us and all people, except for Jesus Christ.

Original Sin Defined

The Article begins by denying a false understanding of original sin. Original sin is not a matter of our being influenced by bad company. as if the Fall of Adam and Eve in the Garden was just a moral example. This view does not go deep enough into who we are; it only deals with what we do. In short, it deals with sinning but not with sinfulness. Pelagius (3rd-4th c. AD) taught that in the Fall we emerged undamaged in our nature, so we could simply stop sinning if we chose to do so; exhortation is all we need. That superficial view is not in accord with the Bible and was decisively refuted by St. Augustine. It is a heresy.

The Article defines original sin as a corruption of our nature. At this point we need to make an important point to avoid a misunderstanding. Our nature was created righteous and perfect. Original sin is the contamination of something great and good, a gift of God. This is important because when something good has been corrupted, it can be restored to its goodness. If it is created bad, there is nothing that can be restored. And further, if we say God created us bad, we demean God, for God does not create bad things.

Original Sin Transmitted to All

It is one thing for Adam and Eve to fall, but how does that affect us? The Article says that original sin "is naturally engendered in the offspring of Adam." This is a genetic model. As parents pass on physical characteristics to their children via DNA, so Adam and Eve, from the origin of the human race, passed on to us a corrupt nature, which is the meaning of *original* sin. This is, of course, an analogy. We are trying to understand something spiritual which is mysterious. However, the proof is in the pudding. We are all Adam's children. Any look at world history, or at oneself, verifies the universality of sinfulness and sinful actions. There are only two options: either we all are essentially bad by nature and beyond all hope, or we are something good that is corrupted. The Bible clearly takes the second view.

The Twofold Result of Original Sin

The first result of original sin is that there is a war in our selves between the flesh and the spirit. Here the "flesh" is not simply physical flesh but a powerful orientation of our hearts that inclines us to succumb to inordinate desires and passions, including inordinate physical desires. The spirit is that part of us that thinks, wills, and consciously relates to God, others, self, and the world. Scripture often refers to it as our heart. These parts of our nature are in conflict with each other. St. Paul puts it this way: "I see in my members another law waging war against the law of my mind and making me captive to the law of sin that dwells in my members" (Rom 7:23).

The second result is that from birth on, we stand under the judgment of God and deserve His condemnation. It is because of this dire condition before God that salvation by God in Christ is so necessary. We are created to love God with all our soul, strength, and mind and our neighbor as ourselves. But, as fallen sinners, we do not primarily love Him who loves us and whose love is meant to flow through us back to Himself and out to our neighbors. World history is the result and hell its destiny.

Original Sin in the Saved

This part of the Article may come as a surprise to many readers, but it is important to grasp if we are not to have false expectations. When we come to salvation in Christ, original sin is weakened but not removed. The inner fight in us continues until our death or the Second Coming of Christ. There is no moral perfectionism in the biblical view of salvation. Condemnation is removed, but living the godly life never becomes easy or perfect.

The Holy Spirit unites us to Christ and brings us effective help in the inner fight. St. Paul puts it this way: "Work out your salvation with fear and trembling, for it is God who is at work within you to will and to do His good pleasure" (Phil 2:12). In Christ, we can live better lives in the Spirit than we could on our own. We can grow in the new life in Christ, as the Spirit lives within us and as we are assisted by our life in the Church.

Prayer

Set us free, loving Father, from the bondage of our sins and in your goodness and mercy give us the liberty of that abundant life which you have made known to us in our Savior Jesus Christ, who lives and reigns with you in the unity of the Holy Spirit, one God, now and forever. *Amen.*

Scripture Texts

Genesis 6:5 "The Lord saw that the wickedness of man was great in the earth and that every intention of the thoughts of his heart was only evil continually."

1 John 1:8-10 "If we say we have no sin, we deceive ourselves, and the truth is not in us. If we confess our sins, he is faithful and just to forgive us our sins and to cleanse us from all unrighteousness. If we say we have not sinned, we make him a liar, and his word is not in us."

Questions for Discussion

1. If we inherit a corrupt nature from Adam, how can God hold us accountable for our sinning?
2. Have you experienced the inner battle of flesh and spirit, and the help of the Holy Spirit preventing you from a specific sinful act?
3. Can we do anything perfectly?

Article 10

Of Free Will

> The condition of Man after the fall of Adam is such, that he cannot turn and prepare himself, by his own natural strength and good works, to faith; and calling upon God. Wherefore we have no power to do good works pleasant and acceptable to God, without the grace of God by Christ preventing us, that we may have a good will, and working with us, when we have that good will.

This Article has two main points: 1. all fallen human beings are in bondage, with our wills incapable of turning to God in love, repentance, and faith; and 2. God, knowing our bondage, gives us the initial grace to turn to him and having come to Him, He gives us the sustaining grace to walk in His ways.

The Bondage of the Will

How are we to understand the bondage of our will? How does sin hold us captive?

First, we need to consider what we mean by "our will." Our will is us deciding whether and how to act or not to act in any given situation. We have the capacity and the necessity to make decisions and we are accountable for these decisions, for they are our choosing and our doing. Our will is guided by our worldview, our character, and most fundamentally by the inclination of our heart, the center of our selves.

Now we must face the sad truth that according to Scripture, our heart is inclined to enthrone itself, to be in charge of our own lives. Luther called it the *cor incurvatus in se*, "the heart turned in upon itself." St. Augustine called it our "disordered affections." We ourselves are sitting where God should sit, upon the throne of our lives. Therefore, we cannot love God with all our heart, strength, and mind, for that position is taken. We cannot love our neighbor as we love ourselves. Our will is bound captive to the self-exalting pride of our fallen hearts. We cannot change our heart because we do not have the heart for it. Of ourselves we cannot be who we are created to be. We need a new heart. Mere exhortation will not transform us.

The consequences of this bondage are earth-shattering. Since God is in fact the Lord of all creation, including us, our lordly decisions put us at odds with God and under His final judgment, and in turn we find ourselves at odds with our neighbors as well. That is the reason for the difficulty of marriage, for tensions in society, and for the wars that haunt the human story, not to mention eternal condemnation as our destiny.

Conversion and Sanctification

But God was not content to leave us bound in sin. In His grace He comes to the rescue. The term "grace" in this Article, and often in Scripture, refers to God's active favor shown to those who not only do not deserve His love or favor but who deserve His final condemnation.

In our conversion, God's grace goes ahead ("prevents" has the meaning of "precedes") to give us a new heart, a new primary inclination of our central self. In theology this is often referred to as regeneration, or rebirth. Regeneration occurs when the Holy Spirit breaks the bondage of sin and opens us to respond to the Gospel: "And the Lord opened the heart of Lydia to attend to the preaching of Paul" (Acts 16:14). His grace leads us to receive the Gospel by repentance and faith.

In sanctification, which is our growing more and more like

Christ, God's grace, applied by the Holy Spirit indwelling us, sustains us in our intention to obey God's will in all things. God will never let us go nor leave us on our own apart from His sustaining grace. That is surely good news.

Prayer

Heavenly Father, you have made us for yourself, and our hearts are restless until they rest in you: Look with compassion upon the heartfelt desires of your servants, and purify our disordered affections, that we may behold your eternal glory in the face of Christ Jesus; who lives and reigns with you and the Holy Spirit, one God, for ever and ever. *Amen.*

Scripture Texts

Jeremiah 17:9 "The heart is deceitful above all things, and desperately sick; who can understand it?"

1 Corinthians 15:10 "But by the grace of God I am what I am, and his grace toward me was not in vain. On the contrary, I worked harder than any of them, though it was not I, but the grace of God that is with me."

Questions for Discussion

1. What are some of the external limitations that bind you and keep you from doing what you might want to do? How do these limitations differ from internal conflicts that keep you from loving God above all else in your life?
2. Is there anything you can do to deserve the grace of God?
3. Describe some of the ways you have experienced the grace of God at work in your life.

Article 11

Of the Justification of Man

We are accounted righteous before God, only for the merit of our Lord and Saviour Jesus Christ by Faith, and not for our own works or deservings. Wherefore, that we are justified by Faith only, is a most wholesome Doctrine, and very full of comfort, as more largely is expressed in the Homily of Justification.

If we fail to get this Article right, we will have lost our ability to read the Scriptures correctly or to understand the Christian Faith. This Article is true and central and must be held by Anglicans and any other community that calls itself Christian. Herein lies the heart of the Good News of Christ. Luther referred to it as "the article by which the church stands or falls," and all the major Churches of the Reformation concurred.

Article 11 has three points: 1. we are accounted (or reckoned) righteous by God for the merit of our Lord and Savior Jesus Christ; 2. we receive this righteousness or merit of Jesus Christ through faith and not by anything we have done or can do; and 3. this doctrine is very full of comfort.

Accounted Righteous

The background of "accounted" is primarily legal, but it also is used in commercial dealings (think "credited"). Before the law we have an account and a judge. For us to be accounted righteous, the judge must declare us righteous or innocent of any charges against us and hence in good standing in society. In commercial dealings our account can have no debt. The amazing thing is that God declares us, sinners that we are, to be justified, innocent, in good standing with Himself. In Christ, our account, despite our debts, is rich beyond measure.

The question arises, on what basis can a holy God declare us sinners to be righteous or justified in His sight? Certainly not based on *our* merit, because before God we have none and are justly condemned. It is based on Jesus' merit, His righteousness transferred to our account. His birth, His righteous life lived, His sacrificial death upon the Cross, His victory over death in the Resurrection, are all credited by God to us who are united to Christ Jesus by His election and our faith. Our justification or right standing with God rests only on Christ's Work and not at all on anything we have done or could do. Here we have one of the famous *"sola's"* of the Reformation. In particular, Christ's righteousness alone (*sola Christi*) is the basis for our salvation.

Justification through Faith Alone

God does not account everyone willy-nilly as justified on the basis of Christ's merit. He justifies those who are related to Jesus as Savior and Lord through faith, not through our being good or keeping the law. It is through faith alone and not through any works on our part that we receive God's verdict of justified in His sight. Here is another of the Reformation sola's: *sola fidei*, "by faith alone."

Faith in relation to justification or salvation is trusting God, trusting His Person in all His attributes (see Article 1), trusting His work for us in Christ as fully sufficient for our salvation and trusting Him in His Word to us in the Gospel. Faith arises in us in response to God revealed to us in Christ.

Faith involves repentance. To repent is to turn *from* sin. Faith is to turn *toward* Christ for His forgiveness and eternal life. We can only face in one direction. To turn to Christ is necessarily to turn away from sin at the same time. We cannot sincerely do one, turn to Christ, and not the other, turn from sin, because they are going in two opposite directions.

Someone may ask: "since repentance and faith are what we do, why is this not a good work by which we earn our salvation?" There are several reasons why we cannot regard faith in Christ as our meritorious good work.

First, faith in Christ is the receiving of a totally undeserved gift. No one takes credit for receiving an utterly precious gift.

Second, faith is not a good work because our faith and repentance are imperfect and just like all our doings must be covered by the righteousness of Christ.

And lastly, our faith is not a good work because faith is itself a gift of God, as the Apostle Paul makes clear. "For by grace you have been saved by faith. And this is not your own doing: it is the gift of God, not as the result of works, so that no one may boast" (Eph 2:8-9). Paul continues: "For we are his workmanship, created in Christ Jesus for good works, which God prepared beforehand, that we should walk in." Having made clear that faith is a gift of God and we are His workmanship, the Apostle speaks of what we are enabled to do, good works and how they follow justification and therefore are in no way the basis of justification.

Full of Comfort

We are, as fallen sinners, utterly beyond self-help and under condemnation. Our works and even our faith are no basis for a right relationship with God. Trusting in God's saving gift in Christ and not in anything we do, is full of comfort because of the greatness and goodness of God. He is the Savior, and we are in good hands forever, despite however sinful we are and whatever sins we may have done or may still commit. That is comfort indeed! As the old hymn puts it, "Blessed assurance, Jesus is mine! Oh, what a foretaste of glory divine!"

Prayer

Grant us, O Lord, we pray, the spirit to think and do always those things that are right, that we who can do no good thing apart from you, may by you be enabled to live according to your will; through Jesus Christ our Lord, who lives and reigns with you and the Holy Spirit, one God, forever and ever. *Amen.*

Scripture Texts

Romans 4:23-25 "But the words 'it was counted to him' were not written for his sake alone, but for ours also. It will be counted unto us who believe in him who raised from the dead Jesus our Lord, who was delivered up for our trespasses and raised for our justification."

John 1:12 "But to all who did receive him, who believed in his name, he gave the right to become the children of God."

Questions for Discussion

1. Compose a modern parable illustrating God's accounting you as righteous.
2. What is the difference between belief that and belief in?
3. Do you really believe that nothing you can do affects your justification in Christ? Why is this hard to believe?

Article 12

Of Good Works

Albeit that Good Works, which are the fruits of Faith, and follow after Justification, cannot put away our sins, and endure the severity of God's judgment; yet are they pleasing and acceptable to God in Christ, and do spring out necessarily of a true and lively Faith insomuch that by them a lively Faith may be as evidently known as a tree discerned by the fruit.

The Article makes four brief points: 1. good works flow from justification; 2. good works cannot put away our sins; 3. good works are pleasing to God; and 4, good works inevitably spring from sincere faith.

Good Works Flowing from Justification.

Unconverted men and women define a good work in various ways as something you achieve, from climbing up the corporate ladder to raising perfect children for an Ivy League college. These works in themselves are not bad, but the motive behind them is often self-love. The Article, following Scripture, speaks instead of good works as "fruit of the Spirit" or "faith working through love." A good work requires a good motive; it must be done with a good heart as well as conforming to God's revealed will. When defining a good deed, one does well to stick with loving God supremely and the neighbor as oneself, and with specific instructions found in Scripture viewed in the light of Christ.

Why does the Article state that good works "follow" justification? The answer is that our good works are not the basis of justification but are the fruit of faith and justification. They follow or arise within the justified life in Christ. And they are done with the help of the indwelling Holy Spirit.

Forgiveness of Sin through Faith Alone

In justifying us through Christ, God has already reconciled us to Himself and put away our sins. There is no need for us to try to do what He has done. As the Apostle Paul puts it: "There is therefore, now, no condemnation to those who are in Christ Jesus" (Rom 8:1). Hence our good works, however noble, must never be thought to be the basis of our relationship with God. This point is spiritually crucial due to the tendency in all of us to come to think, consciously or unconsciously, that our good behavior is foundational in our being right with God. This tendency must be discerned and rejected, for it compromises the Gospel, weakens our confidence, and dishonors God.

Good Works Pleasing to God

While our best works are imperfect, God as our Father is pleased to see our efforts to walk in the Spirit and to conform our lives to the character of our Lord, Jesus Christ. In His discipline of us, He will encourage us to grow in grace. As we delight in the efforts of our children and seek to encourage them, much more will our heavenly Father encourage and care for us.

Good Works the Fruit of Sincere Faith

One of the tests of a prophet is, "Do his predictions come true?" The test of a believer is, "Does his life reflect a desire to please God in all things?" This desire and the works that follow from it, come from the heart. They are natural to a renewed heart, and the total absence of them in a person's life raises questions as to the genuineness of his or her faith. For this reason, James warns: "Faith without works is dead" (James 2:26).

United to Christ and indwelt by the Spirit, we can expect the fruit of the Spirit to begin to characterize our lives, and that is a hopeful thought.

Prayer

Thanks be to thee, my Lord Jesus Christ, for all the pains and insults thou hast borne for me, and all the benefits thou hast given me. O most merciful Redeemer, Friend, and Brother: Grant that I may see thee more clearly, love thee more dearly, and follow thee more nearly, day by day. *Amen.*

Scripture Texts

John 15:5 "I am the vine; you are the branches. Whoever abides in me and I in him, he it is that bears much fruit, for apart from me you can do nothing."

Romans 8:9 "You, however, are not in the flesh but in the Spirit, if in fact the Spirit of God indwells you. Anyone who does not have the Spirit of Christ does not belong to him."

Questions for Discussion

1. How would you define a good work? Do you ever consciously do anything to please God?
2. Why is it essential that we believe that good works "follow after" justification?
3. Why are our good works, done in faith, necessary?

Article 13

Of Works before Justification

Works done before the grace of Christ, and the Inspiration of his Spirit, are not pleasant to God, forasmuch as they spring not of faith in Jesus Christ; neither do they make men meet to receive grace, or (as the School-authors say) deserve grace of congruity: yea rather, for that they are not done as God hath willed and commanded them to be done, we doubt not but they have the nature of sin.

There are two points in this Article: 1. works before justification are not pleasing to God; 2. such works do not make us worthy to receive grace from God but are in fact sinful.

Works before Justification Not Pleasing to God

The works that are unpleasing to God are done by people who have not come to faith in Christ. The inner work of the Spirit has not yet been given to them nor are they responding to God in faith and love. Hence their efforts to do good works, even those that are objectively commendable, are disconnected from the new creation that God has brought into the world through Jesus. They are not in God's eyes "good works."

False Teaching that Works Prepare Us for Justification

During the medieval or "scholastic" period, it was widely taught that one must do his or her part by seeking God by various good works in order to earn the right for us to receive grace from God. We do our "congruous" part not aided by Him, and then God, in recognition of what we have done, will do His part and give us the grace of salvation. This makes salvation dependent on our taking the initiative and contributing something to our salvation. This teaching is rejected by this Article, because it is contrary to Scripture and denies the bondage of the will and the free grace of God.

It is humbling to realize that we can in no way earn our salvation in Christ. Seeking God is not in and of itself sinful; indeed, it is enjoined in Scripture. But believing that what we do earns us credit from God is sinful. There is nothing that we sinners can do to make God our debtor in any sense.

Salvation is His free, amazing, and entirely undeserved gift to us. The initiative to save us belongs entirely to Him, for which gift we give Him our deepest thanks.

Prayer

O God of peace, who hast taught us that in returning and rest we shall be saved, in quietness and in confidence shall be our strength: By the might of thy Spirit lift us, we pray, to your presence, where we may be still and know that thou art God; through Jesus Christ our Lord. *Amen.*

Scripture Texts

John 3:36 "Whoever believes in the Son has eternal life; whoever does not obey the Son shall not see life, but the wrath of God remains on him."

Romans 3:23 "For all have sinned and fall short of the glory of God."

Questions for Discussion

1. Why is a kind act done by an unbeliever to impress God not pleasing to God?
2. Consider the case of the rich young ruler who came to Jesus and said, "What must I do to inherit eternal life?" (Luke 18:18-23). How did Jesus challenge him?

Article 14

Of Works of Supererogation

> Voluntary Works besides, over and above, God's Commandments, which they call Works of Supererogation, cannot be taught without arrogancy and impiety: for by them men do declare, that they do not only render unto God as much as they are bound to do, but that they do more for his sake, than of bounden duty is required: whereas Christ saith plainly When ye have done all that are commanded to you, say, We are unprofitable servants.

This Article makes but one point. It states that there are no supplemental "works of supererogation" beyond faith and love that please God. God demands our all, our "bounden duty and service," in life and in whatever vocation to which we may be called to glorify God with all that is within us.

Some theologians in the unreformed Western Catholic Church taught that while all Christians are called to obey God in the ordinary patterns of life, the monastic vows of poverty, obedience and chastity (i.e., celibacy) were acts above and beyond what God expects of us. These works of "supererogation" are more than God *asks* us to do. They earn merit in the sight of God, and they add additional merit to the Church's "treasury of merit" that can be applied to souls in purgatory (see Article 22). This teaching is to be rejected.

The Article seals this point by referring to Jesus' own teaching. When the disciples asked Him to "increase our faith," he replied that there is nothing a servant can do beyond his duty to his Master: "So you also, when you have done all that you were

Part Three: Salvation in Christ

commanded, say, 'We are unworthy servants; we have only done what was our duty'" (Luke 17:5-10).

Prayer

O Lord God Almighty, it is our duty and our joy, always and everywhere to serve you and to give thanks to you. So, move in our hearts by your Holy Spirit that we may ever do the same, through Jesus Christ, our Savior in whose name we pray. *Amen.*

Scripture Text

Luke 17:10 "So you also, when you have done all you were commanded, say 'We are unworthy servants; we have only done what was our duty.'"

Questions for Discussion

1. Do you think of clergy or missionaries as especially holy? How does this notion fit with the idea of the priesthood of all believers?
2. Discuss the words of the General Thanksgiving in the Prayer Book: "Give us such an awareness of your mercies that with truly thankful hearts we may show forth your praise, not only with our lips, but in our lives, by giving up our selves to your service.

Article 15

Of Christ alone without Sin

Christ in the truth of our nature was made like unto us in all things, sin only except, from which he was clearly void, both in his flesh, and in his spirit. He came to be the Lamb without spot, who, by sacrifice of himself once made, should take away the sins of the world; and sin (as Saint John saith) was not in him. But all we the rest, although baptized and born again in Christ, yet offend in many things; and if we say we have no sin, we deceive ourselves, and the truth is not in us.

This Article makes two points: 1. only the incarnate Christ was and is without sin; and 2. all the rest of us continue to sin, whether we are born-again Christians or not.

Only Christ without Sin

Not everyone regarded Jesus as sinless. The Jewish authorities accused Him of the high crime of blasphemy for claiming God as His Father. The Romans crucified Him as an insurrectionist. The Pharisees considered Him a lawbreaker who associated with sinners. But His disciples, those who knew Him best, considered Him to be the sinless Son of the living God.

The evidence of His sinlessness is diverse. His miraculous conception by the Holy Spirit in the womb of Mary, His remarkable miracles of healing, exorcism and authority over nature, His teaching us to repent but never repenting or seeking forgiveness for Himself, the voice from Heaven at the transfiguration, his death and His Resurrection with the Father's approval, all point to his unique sinlessness.

This Article highlights one evidence of His sinlessness, which is His having come as the Lamb of God to take away the sins of the world (John 1:29,36). In order to qualify as our sin-bearer on our behalf, He needed to be sinless. In this regard, He fulfilled and ended the Old Testament sacrifices for sin which required an unblemished animal, which by themselves could not bring a final atonement (Heb 10:4). Therefore, the sacrifice for our sins required a human sinless substitute for us, Who, as human, is also representative of us all.

The Ubiquity of Sin

Once again, we are reminded that everyone, except Christ, is a sinner who sins before and after conversion. Doctrines of perfectionism are contrary to the Scripture and to the Anglican understanding of the Faith. We all may be saints, but we are at the same time forgiven and justified sinners in Christ. We are, as Martin Luther famously said, "simultaneously just and sinners" (*simul justus et peccator*). Perfection comes only in glory.

Prayer

Stir up your power, O Lord, and with great might come among us; and as we are sorely hindered by our sins from running the race that is set before us, let your bountiful grace and mercy speedily help and deliver us; through Jesus Christ our Lord, to whom with you and the Holy Spirit, be honor and glory, now and forever. *Amen.*

Scripture Texts

1 Peter 2:22 "He committed no sin, neither was deceit found in his mouth."

2 Corinthians 5:21 "For our sake [God] made [Christ] to be sin who knew no sin, so that in him we might become the righteousness of God."

Questions for Discussion

1. How can we be sure that all people are sinful when we do not know the thoughts of the heart?
2. Do you think babies are sinful? In what way?
3. If someone were to ask you how you know that Jesus Christ was sinless, how would you answer?

Article 16

Of Sin after Baptism

> Not every deadly sin willingly committed after Baptism is sin against the Holy Ghost, and unpardonable. Wherefore the grant of repentance is not to be denied to such as fall into sin after Baptism. After we have received the Holy Ghost, we may depart from grace given, and fall into sin, and by the grace of God we may arise again, and amend our lives. And therefore they are to be condemned, which say, they can no more sin as long as they live here, or deny the place of forgiveness to such as truly repent.

The main point of this Article is to make clear the amazing forgiveness of God and our calling to receive, embody and share it.

This Article makes four points: 1. there is an unforgiveable sin; 2. sins committed after baptism are to be forgiven those who sincerely repent; 3. believers who have received the Holy Spirit indwelling in them can fall into a sinful life and still be raised up by the grace of God to renewed faith and amendment of life; and 4. those who claim that Christians can never sin or who deny forgiveness to fallen and repentant Christians are to be condemned.

The Unforgiveable Sin

The Article begins by referring to a dark saying of Jesus that "all sins will be forgiven the children of man, and whatever blasphemies they utter, but whoever blasphemes against the Holy Spirit never has forgiveness but is guilty of an eternal sin" (Mark 3:28-29). Those who are members of God's people are warned against rejecting the work of the Spirit in forgiving others through Christ, and so hardening their hearts that they reject the work that the Spirit is doing in their own hearts.

Sins after Baptism

There was a teaching in the patristic Church that after you were baptized, you could not be forgiven any subsequent sins, however trivial. This led some persons to delay baptism until they were on their deathbed. This harsh attitude speaks of a rigid legalism, a superficial understanding of what sin is, and a lack of trust in the compassion in Christ. We all sin after baptism, for we are far from perfected. Thus, repentance and faith are always open to the contrite heart.

Backsliders Renewed by Grace

Backsliders are those who have fallen away from the faith they once confessed. Even for these, we are to continue to have hope and seek to restore them by repentance, enabled by God's grace. With God all things are possible. The Prayer Book includes a General Confession in every service to remind us that we all need to repent and amend our lives.

Perfectionism Rejected

Some strands of Protestant Christianity have taught that one can live a perfect life in the power of the Spirit. Such an attitude easily slips into judgmentalism and moralism. This part of the Article strongly warns those in the Church who have adopted an unforgiving, ungenerous, and unhopeful spirit and who would cease to seek to win back fallen brothers and sisters. We are to be honest about sin but also to embody and share the forgiveness and grace which is at work in us.

Prayer

Almighty and everlasting God, whose will it is to restore all things in your well-beloved Son, the King of kings and Lord of lords: Mercifully grant that the peoples of the earth, divided and enslaved by sin, may be freed and brought together under his most gracious rule; who lives and reigns with you and the Holy Spirit, one God, now and for ever. *Amen.*

Scripture Texts

Luke 12: 10 "And everyone who speaks a word against the Son of Man will be forgiven, but the one who blasphemes against the Holy Spirit will not be forgiven."

1 John 1: 9 "If we confess our sins, he is faithful and just to forgive us our sins and to cleanse us from all unrighteousness."

Questions for Discussion

1. What, in your opinion, is blasphemy against the Holy Spirit, and why is it unforgiveable?
2. Have you ever been tempted to shun a repentant sinner?
3. Do you have any lapsed friends? If so, what are you doing about it?

Article 17

Of Predestination and Election

Predestination to Life is the everlasting purpose of God, whereby (before the foundations of the world were laid) he hath constantly decreed by his counsel secret to us, to deliver from curse and damnation those whom he hath chosen in Christ out of mankind, and to bring them by Christ to everlasting salvation, as vessels made to honour. Wherefore, they which be endued with so excellent a benefit of God, be called according to God's purpose by his Spirit working in due season: they through Grace obey the calling: they be justified freely: they be made sons of God by adoption: they be made like the image of his only-begotten Son Jesus Christ: they walk religiously in good works, and at length, by God's mercy, they attain to everlasting felicity.

As the godly consideration of Predestination, and our Election in Christ, is full of sweet, pleasant, and unspeakable comfort to godly persons, and such as feel in themselves the working of the Spirit of Christ, mortifying the works of the flesh, and their earthly members, and drawing up their mind to high and heavenly things, as well because it doth greatly establish and confirm their faith of eternal Salvation to be enjoyed through Christ as because it doth fervently kindle their love towards God: So, for curious and carnal persons, lacking the Spirit of Christ, to have continually before their eyes the sentence of God's Predestination, is a most dangerous downfall, whereby the Devil doth thrust them either into desperation, or into wretchlessness of most unclean living, no less perilous than desperation.

Furthermore, we must receive God's promises in such wise, as they be generally set forth to us in Holy Scripture: and, in our doings, that Will of God is to be followed, which we have expressly declared unto us in the Word of God.

This Article sets forth the Anglican understanding of God's sovereign electing grace and the predestination of our eternal souls.

There are three main points in this Article: 1. God chooses ("elects") some men and women to come to Christ and receive everlasting salvation; 2. those who are so chosen or elected are called effectively by the Spirit; 3. God's election of the godly, though a mystery, is a doctrine full of comfort and joy, while it frustrates and angers unbelievers.

God's Election to Salvation

Numerous texts in Scripture speak of God's elect as referring to Israel, the Church, and as referring to individual persons. The Article speaks specifically of "those chosen in Christ," that is, those who respond to the Gospel. While Christ died for the sins of the whole world and God's loves rests on all, His electing some for salvation and bypassing others is clear from Scripture. His "secret counsel" for doing this has not been revealed to us, and speculation on our part is fruitless. For this very reason, we are encouraged to "publish glad tidings" to all peoples and leave the results to God.

We should note that there is no assertion that God chooses some for damnation (double predestination). Election is to life in Christ now and forever. Damnation is solely the result of a person's rejection of the Gospel.

Effective Calling

By the fulness of the atoning work of Christ and the sending of the indwelling Holy Spirit, God effectively leads the elect to their final destination in glory. What God purposes, He accomplishes, without fail.

Mysterious yet Comforting Election

Some people brood over the question of whether they are "elect," or they judge others as clearly headed for hellfire. According to this Article, God intends our election in Christ to be full of joy, gratitude and confidence of our election, and we are not to let the fact that this is full of mystery rob us of the joy of this unspeakable blessing.

This doctrine humbles us, for it puts our salvation entirely in God's hands. It perplexes us, for why does God choose only some and not all? However, this must not lead us to deny or distort the biblical doctrine of election to life, by which we were chosen before we came to faith in Christ and which choice is the godly basis of our faith in Christ.

Meditation on our election in Christ encourages believers but it discourages unbelievers. This doctrine has been called a doctrine for believers only. Bunyan in his *Pilgrim's Progress* put it this way. As the traveler comes to the great gate that leads to the path to the Celestial City, he sees written on the gate "Enter all ye who will" (this is the call of the Gospel to everyone.) Having passed through the gate (and accepted the Gospel), the traveler looks back at the other side of the gate. On it is written: "chosen from before the foundation of the earth." The comfort of this doctrine is for those who have passed through the gate and are on the road to the celestial city. To believe it is a great comfort indeed!

Prayer

O Lord, you never fail to support and govern those whom you bring up in your steadfast love and fear: Keep us, we pray, under your continual protection and providence, and give us a perpetual fear and love of your holy Name; through Jesus Christ our Lord, who lives and reigns with you and the Holy Spirit, one God, forever and ever. *Amen.*

Scripture Texts

Matthew 24:31 "And he will send his angels with a great sound of a trumpet, and they will gather together his elect from the four winds, from one end of the heaven to the other."

John 6:37 "All that the Father gives me will come to me, and whoever comes to me I will never cast out."

1 Thessalonians 5:9 "For God has not destined us for wrath, but to obtain salvation through our Lord Jesus Christ."

Questions for Discussion

1. Do you find that the fact that God chose you for salvation in Christ before you were born, or even before creation, fills you with joy and comfort? Why or why not?
2. Why is it wrong to reject or ignore the doctrine of election?
3. What might be the reasons that people get upset at the doctrine of election to life?
4. Does this Article teach that God predestines some people to hell?

Article 18

Of obtaining eternal Salvation only by the Name of Christ

They also are to be had accursed that presume to say, That every man shall be saved by the Law or Sect which he professeth, so that he be diligent to frame his life according to that Law, and the light of Nature. For Holy Scripture doth set out unto us only the Name of Jesus Christ, whereby men must be saved.

This Article makes two points. 1. people are not saved by sincerely following the world's religions or philosophies; and 2. salvation is found in the Name of Christ alone.

The Dangers of Pluralism in Religion or Philosophy

The view that all religions are salvific if they are held sincerely was being taught at the time of the Reformation and is even more common in our day, going under the name of "pluralism" or "many roads up to the top of the same mountain." Here such views are clearly rejected as being false and unbiblical. Sincerity proves nothing. People are often sincerely wrong. Believing something does not make it true or salvific. People believe all sorts of things and hold mutually contradictory religions and philosophies.

Salvation in Christ Alone

God's revelation in nature is true but it is insufficient for salvation (Rom 1:18-21). It is suppressed by us sinners and interpreted often in erroneous ways. Neither can we be justified by following the Jewish law or any other moral code (Romans, chapter 2). God has offered the fallen race only one "Name" by which we can be saved, that of Jesus Christ (Acts 4:12). Jesus Himself states clearly: "I am the Way, the Truth, and the Life; no one comes to the Father except through me" (John 14:6). God the Son first came to us, making a way to God for us, who are alienated sinners needing a rescue by God. While the gate (Christ alone) is narrow, all are invited. No one who is sincerely desirous of coming to God through Christ is refused. Ask and you shall receive.

Prayer

O God, you have made of one blood all the peoples of the earth, and sent your blessed Son to preach peace to those who are far off and those who are near: Grant that people everywhere may seek after you and find you; bring the nations into your fold; pour out your Spirit upon all flesh; and hasten the coming of your kingdom; through Jesus Christ our Lord. *Amen.*

Scripture Texts

Matthew 7:13 "Enter by the narrow gate. For the gate is wide and the way is easy that leads to destruction, and those who enter by it are many."

Acts 4:12 "And there is salvation in no one else, for there is no other name under heaven given among men by which we must be saved."

Questions for Discussion

1. Is there something about the exclusivity of salvation in Christ alone that bothers you? What is it and why?
2. What reasons would you give to someone that asked you why you believe that Jesus is the only way to a saving relationship with God?

Part Four

The Church, Sacraments, and the Ordained Ministry (Articles 19-36)

This section – "of the Church" – has the largest number of Articles because of differences regarding the church that existed at the time of the Reformation. Justification by faith, as set forth in Scripture, was the linchpin of the Reformation, and that doctrine influences all the Articles including the Articles in this section, but despite that, significant differences remain.

The differences between the Churches were and remain significant. Anglicans, Lutherans, and Reformed (Calvinistic) Churches tended to focus on the application of Jesus' work on the Cross and Resurrection to believers through faith. Belief was not only right doctrine but a personal trust in God known through the Good News of the Gospel. This faith arises in response to the preaching of the Gospel and the sharing of the sacraments. Preaching was considered central by the framers of the Articles, although, sadly, this intention was often not carried out on the ground.

The focus of the Roman Catholic Church was on the Church as a dispenser of the sacraments, which were thought to communicate God's grace automatically (*ex opere operato*) as one partook of them, so long as one was in a sacramental "state of grace" and had not offended God by unconfessed or mortal sin. The whole approach to Christianity was more objective, and the place of human effort was considered to have some merit in the eyes of God.

There was a third loosely related group of smaller Churches usually referred to as Anabaptists, since they did not believe in infant baptism. Their focus was more on the Holy Spirit and His work in the inner life of the Christian, which would produce holiness, peace and caring service to those in need. Some of these Churches wanted to separate themselves from the wider society, and they formed conventicles; others became militaristic or utopian. One familiar group is the Quakers, who rejected the necessity of any of the usual means of grace, such as the preached word or the sacraments, or any need for clergy. Quakers held that as they gathered in quiet, the Spirit would speak to the church through one or more of the members, as the Spirit determined. Unfortunately, many of these groups were persecuted, and none were accepted by the "godly princes" as the official religion in their territories.

In the Articles in this section, you will see how Anglicans came to address these differences in the light of the Gospel, in faithfulness to Holy Scripture and in accord with many of the historic traditions of the Church.

Article 19
Of the Church

The visible Church of Christ is a congregation of faithful men, in which the pure Word of God is preached, and the Sacraments be duly ministered according to Christ's ordinance, in all those things that of necessity are requisite to the same. As the Church of Jerusalem, Alexandria, and Antioch, have erred, so also the Church of Rome hath erred, not only in their living and manner of Ceremonies, but also in matters of Faith.

This Article makes two important points about the church: 1. it defines the marks of a visible Church; and 2. it notes that all Churches, including the Roman Catholic Church, err in doctrine and practices.

Marks of the Visible Church

The visible Church is defined as a "congregation of faithful men." The words "congregation" and "visible" need a brief clarification. "Men" of course refers to men and women.

The word "congregation" can refer to the local congregation (we'll use lower case "c" for these) and also to a group of churches in an area or with a common tradition (we'll use upper case "C" for these). Some Churches claimed an ancient, "apostolic" foundation or "See," such as Jerusalem, Alexandria, Antioch and Rome. The Churches of the Reformation, including the Church of England, did not claim such a foundation, though Canterbury was an early see, and they argued that no claim to authority was proof against error, i.e., false teaching.

The local church is a manifestation of a wider family of Churches, sometimes called a "denomination" or "communion." They all have the same spiritual DNA, so to speak. A parish church, for instance, may be part of the Anglican Church in North America, which is part of the worldwide Anglican Communion, which in turn confesses membership in the "one holy catholic and apostolic Church." The Article makes clear that the primary life of the Church is in the local gathered community.

The word "visible" distinguishes a visible Church from the Church in heaven, all those saved by Christ (Heb 12:22-24), which we cannot see. "Invisible" also points to the communion between all faithful Christians, the elect, in all the Churches, as distinguished from nominal Christians (in name only). The Church in this sense is invisible because we cannot easily distinguish between the faithful and the nominal members, which Jesus called the wheat and the tares.

There was then and there is now a need to set forth the visible characteristics or "marks" that a congregation of people must exhibit if they are to be recognized as a visible expression of the universal or "catholic" Church. Not all groups who refer to themselves as Christian have these marks; one thinks of the cults and these days of some parts of the historic Churches which have fallen into serious heresy or immorality.

What are these marks? The Article names two explicitly. The first mark is the preaching and teaching of the pure Word of God, that is, preaching the Gospel in accordance with the clear teaching of Scripture. Faith arises and is sustained in response to the Gospel, and therefore preaching the Gospel must have a central place in the Church's life.

The second mark is the faithful celebration or "administration" of the sacraments of Holy Baptism and Holy Communion, as Christ instituted them. The sacraments too are Gospel-centered and "declare" the Gospel to the congregation gathered.

There is a third implicit mark, church discipline, which ensures that the first two marks are being carried out faithfully. Although this third mark is not cited in this Article, it is presupposed by it and is cited in the *Book of Homilies* (see the Homily on Whitsunday), which is cited in Article 35 as authoritative for Anglicans.

2. The Fallibility of All Churches

Sin has its effect on the Church as well as the individual. Just as no Christian is without sin and perfection waits for the Second Coming of Christ, so also no Church or tradition is infallible, however ancient and widespread it is.

There can be little doubt that this assertion was aimed at the Roman Catholic Church and its doctrine of the infallibility of the Pope and many of its other binding rules that led to excommunication and even death. Of course, the Article applies more widely, including us in our time. We all need to be ready to test what we believe with a fresh reading of the Scriptures, which is God's Word written.

Prayer

Almighty and everlasting God, you govern all things in heaven and on earth: Mercifully hear our prayers, and grant that in our congregation the pure Word of God may be preached and the sacraments duly administered. Strengthen and confirm the faithful; protect and guide the children; visit and relieve the sick; turn and soften the wicked; arouse the careless; recover the fallen; restore the penitent; remove all hindrances to the advancement of your truth; and bring us all to be of one heart and mind within your holy Church, to the honor and glory of your Name, through Jesus Christ our Lord. *Amen.*

Scripture Texts

Acts 2:42 "And they devoted themselves to the apostles' teaching and fellowship, to the breaking of bread and the prayers."

1 Corinthians 12:13 "For in one Spirit we were all baptized into one body-Jews or Greeks, slaves or free-and all were made to drink of one Spirit."

Revelation 2:1,4-5 "To the angel of the church in Ephesus write: . . . 'I have this against you, that you have abandoned the love you had at first. Remember therefore from where you have fallen; repent, and do the works you did at first. If not, I will come to you and remove your lampstand from its place, unless you repent.'"

Questions for Discussion

1. Would you say that your congregation has the marks of a visible Church? What about your denomination?
2. Who in your congregation exercises discipline over the preaching and the administration of the sacraments? What about your denomination?
3. Why is the Article so certain that all Churches (congregations and denominations) err?

Article 20

Of the Authority of the Church

The Church hath power to decree Rites or Ceremonies, and authority in Controversies of Faith: and yet it is not lawful for the Church to ordain any thing that is contrary to God's Word written, neither may it so expound one place of Scripture, that it be repugnant to another. Wherefore, although the Church be a witness and a keeper of Holy Writ, yet, as it ought not to decree any thing against the same, so besides the same ought it not to enforce any thing to be believed for necessity of Salvation.

There was a difference of view among the English Reformers as to how the sufficiency of Scripture applied to the authority of the Church of England and its parishes. Some Anglicans, often called "non-conformists" or "puritans," believed that *all* Christian doctrine, morals and church order must be prescribed in Scripture. Other Anglicans argued that Scripture's prime aim was "salvation" and that many secondary matters (*adiaphora*) should be left open to disagreement and that the Church of England had discretionary authority in many matters of church order and worship so long as their content was not contrary to the Scriptures. This second view was and is the prevailing Anglican view.

This Article teaches:1. the Church has authority over rites, ceremonies and doctrinal controversies in secondary matters; 2. the Church's authority is under the authority of Scripture; 3. Scripture is harmonious; and 4. nothing may be added to the Gospel as necessary for salvation.

Part Four: The Church, Sacraments, and the Ordained Ministry

The Church's Authority

Our understanding of the Faith is meant to be growing, and there are places where a fresh reading of Scripture may show us that we have erred in our understanding. The same is true for a denomination. So, the Church has the authority and obligation to improve or revise its doctrinal standards when necessary. It also has the authority to set forth its common rites and ceremonies, such as Anglicans have done in the Book of Common Prayer and Hymnal. Clergy in Anglican churches vow to uphold Scripture and the fundamental Articles of Religion, but they also vow to obey the Prayer Book, church rules (canons), and the bishops. They are not free just to "do their own thing."

The Church under the Authority of Scripture

The Church's doctrine, rites and ceremonies must all be in agreement with the teaching of the Holy Scriptures. This is even more important because of their repeated use in the life and worship of the congregation. Such repetition shapes the memory and mind of the members thereof. If people sense a disconnect between the teaching or preaching and the reading of the Bible, they will lose confidence either in the Scripture or the Church. At the same time, the Article leaves room for differences among Churches, so long as they are not "contrary" to Scripture.

The Harmony of Scripture

While the 66 books of the Scriptures were written by various human authors over a long period of time, they are the product of one Divine Mind, and God does not contradict Himself (2 Tim 2:13). Therefore, the Church may not interpret particular texts as though they contradict one another but should seek to reconcile apparent differences. For instance, it cannot teach Jesus is the only Way to the Father and also that there are other Ways. If specific texts appear to us to contradict one another, the fault lies with our understanding and challenges us to dig deeper.

Dangers of Adding to Scripture

Because Scripture is sufficient for salvation, it is not the Church's prerogative to set other requirements for salvation. These have already been set by God in the New Testament Gospel: "Repent and believe in the Gospel and you will be saved." This part of the Article was added because the Anglican Reformers believed that the Church of Rome and the various Anabaptist churches had added on to the plain teaching of the Bible. It remains a danger for us all to equate the distinctives of our denomination with God's requirements for salvation.

Prayer

Gracious Father, we pray for your holy Catholic Church: fill it with all truth, in all truth with all peace; where it is corrupt, purify it; where it is in error, direct it; where in anything it is amiss, reform it; where it is right, strengthen it; where it is in want, provide for it; where it is divided, reunite it; for the sake of Jesus Christ your Son, our Savior. *Amen.*

Scripture Texts

Galatians 1:9 "As we have said before, so now I say again: If anyone is preaching to you a gospel contrary to the one you received, let him be accursed."

1 Timothy 6:3 "If anyone teaches a different doctrine and does not agree with the sound words of our Lord Jesus Christ and the teaching that accords with godliness, he is puffed up with conceit and understands nothing."

Questions for Discussion

1. Why is a Prayer Book a great advantage for the worship of the Church?
2. Is there any limitation to the number and kind of rites the Church should decree?
3. Can you think of any biblical teachings that are hard to harmonize with one another?

Article 21

Of the Authority of General Councils

General Councils may not be gathered together without the commandment and will of Princes. And when they be gathered together, (forasmuch as they be an assembly of men, whereof all be not governed with the Spirit and Word of God,) they may err, and sometimes have erred, even in things pertaining unto God. Wherefore things ordained by them as necessary to salvation have neither strength nor authority, unless it may be declared that they be taken out of holy Scripture.

As noted under Article 6, Anglicans have honored the four General or Ecumenical Councils of the first five centuries and the Creeds which emerged from them; they formulated the doctrines of the Trinity and the Two Natures of Christ. In subsequent centuries, Eastern (Orthodox) and Western (Catholic) Churches convened and recognized other councils as authoritative.

This Article makes three further points about these councils: 1. General Councils must be properly convened; 2. all church councils are subject to error; 3. where General Councils have erred, they have no binding authority.

Convening General Councils

The first General Councils were convened by Christian Roman emperors giving them a worldwide "ecumenical" authority. When the 21st Article was written, Protestant Churches were located in countries headed by a "godly prince," who determined which church was official or permitted in his country. On the other hand, the Roman Catholic Church claimed that the Pope alone had authority over the Christian church. His authority was challenged by the Eastern and the Protestant Churches. This situation made it impossible to gather a truly ecumenical council. Now that Western society has become increasingly secular and democratic and Rome continues to claim papal authority, it is highly unlikely that another General Council will be possible for the foreseeable future.

The Fallibility of Church Councils

In principle, church councils gather to interpret Scripture and invoke the Holy Spirit, as happened at the first Jerusalem Council in Acts. However, as assemblies of fallen and fallible men, they are not infallible.

The Protestant Reformers refused to accept the absolute authority of any council, even the first four, apart from its conformity with Scripture, which is the supreme authority. The Anglican position is that even the Reformation confessions are subject to further reformation ("reformed and ever reforming"). Perfection awaits the Second Coming of Christ.

The Limits of General Councils

The Article is opposed to the Eastern Orthodox position that General Councils have not erred. It also rejects the Roman Catholic position that its councils are without error. Even General Councils are to be corrected by Scripture, and Churches should continually check the scriptural accuracy of their conciliar tradition. Anglicans are serious about the authority of Scripture, rightly interpreted. At the same time, the Articles' approval of the four Ecumenical Councils should weigh in their favor.

The few ongoing creedal questions, e.g., the "filioque clause" in the Nicene Creed (the Spirit proceeding from the Father alone or from the Father and the Son) derive in part from different passages in Scripture (cf. John 15:26; 20:22).

Prayer

Gracious and ever-living Father, you have given the Holy Spirit to abide with us forever: Bless, we pray, with the Holy Spirit's grace and presence, the Bishops, Priests, Deacons, and all the Laity who assemble in your Name; that your Church, being preserved in true faith and godly discipline, may fulfill the will of him who loved her and gave himself for her, your Son Jesus Christ our Savior; who now lives and reigns with you and the same Spirit, one God, now and forever. *Amen.*

Scripture Text

Acts 15:2 "And after Paul and Barnabas had no small dissension and debate with them, Paul and Barnabas and some of the others were appointed to go up to Jerusalem to the apostles and the elders about this question." (This was the first Jerusalem Council)

Questions for Discussion

1. Since church councils can err, why should we bother reading and repeating their creeds and confessions?
2. Every ten years since 1867, Anglican Bishops from around the world have gathered to take counsel and to speak to issues facing the wider Church. In 1998, this Lambeth Conference passed a Resolution upholding biblical teaching on opposite-sex marriage and singleness as the only biblical norm for the church. Was this Resolution consistent with Article 21?

Part Four: The Church, Sacraments, and the Ordained Ministry

Article 22

Of Purgatory

> The Romish Doctrine concerning Purgatory, Pardons, Worshipping and Adoration, as well of Images as of Relics, and also Invocation of Saints, is a fond thing, vainly invented, and grounded upon no warranty of Scripture, but rather repugnant to the Word of God.

Having established that Churches and Councils can err, Article 22 proceeds to detail doctrines and practices of Rome which it considers unbiblical, false, and dangerous to the Faith.

This Article teaches three things: 1. the Roman Catholic Church teaches practices that are contrary to Holy Scripture; 2. purgatory and related pardons is superstitious; 3. worshiping images and relics and invoking the saints is idolatrous.

Roman Catholic Errors

The Reformers not only disagreed with some of the doctrines and practices of the Roman Catholic Church, but they believed they were false ("vain"), superstitious ("fond") and dangerous to true religion as revealed in Scripture. At the same time, Rome was formulating its response at the Council of Trent, which declared the Anglican Articles to be heretical. While there has been progress over the last century in dialogues between Roman Catholics and Protestants, Rome has never renounced Trent nor answered the objections in these Articles.

Purgatory and Pardons

Purgatory and pardons are related. Purgatory is taught to be a place to which members of the Church in a state of grace go upon death, but who need to suffer punishment for sins not sufficiently covered by the usual practice of confession and the assigned acts of repentance. When this suffering is done, and it could take thousands and thousands of years, the sufferer is able to enter heaven. The idea of pardons, years off the time of serious suffering in purgatory, is supported by the notion of a "treasury of merit," gathered from all the works of supererogation (see Article 14), which the Church can apply to a suffering individual in purgatory. This entire calculus has no basis in Scripture and is contrary to the sufficiency of the Cross that gives us all the pardon we need.

Idolatrous Practices

Despite the strong Old Testament emphasis on the invisibility of God and the Commandment against graven images, there grew a tendency in the early church to revere images of the saints (icons) and the remains (relics) of the martyrs. This reverence later developed into practices of worshiping and displaying images and relics, which led to superstition and potentially to idolatry. While recalling the examples of the saints and martyrs is commendable, invocation of the saints is a misdirection of prayer, which we are to address to God, or to one of the Persons of the Trinity. There is no scriptural mandate for talking to the dead, even to our loved ones who have died in Christ.

While Anglicans differ on how to define "Romish" doctrine and practices, the Articles are clear about the danger of all religious practices that contradict Scripture.

Prayer

O Almighty God, you pour out on all who desire it the spirit of grace and of supplication: Deliver us, when we draw near to you, from coldness of heart and wanderings of mind, that with steadfast thoughts and kindled affections we may worship you in spirit and in truth; through Jesus Christ our Lord. *Amen.*

Scripture Texts

1 Corinthians 10:7 "Do not be idolators as some of them were [the Golden Calf], as it is written, 'The people sat down to eat and drink and rose up to play.'"

Romans 8:1-4 "There is therefore now no condemnation for those who are in Christ Jesus. For the law of the Spirit of life has set you free in Christ Jesus from the law of sin and death. For God has done what the law, weakened by the flesh, could not do. By sending his own Son in the likeness of sinful flesh and for sin, he condemned sin in the flesh, in order that the righteous requirement of the law might be fulfilled by us, who walk not according to the flesh but according to the Spirit."

Questions for Discussions

1. Do you think this Article is too condemnatory? Why not let our fellow Christians in the Eastern and Roman Catholic Churches engage in these practices?
2. Can there be such a thing as a "treasury of merit"? What makes such a notion spiritually dangerous?

Article 23

Of Ministering in the Congregation

It is not lawful for any man to take upon him the office of public preaching, or ministering the Sacraments in the Congregation, before he be lawfully called, and sent to execute the same. And those we ought to judge lawfully called and sent, which be chosen and called to this work by men who have public authority given unto them in the Congregation, to call and send Ministers into the Lord's vineyard.

This Article makes two points: 1. ordained ministers must be lawfully called and sent; and 2. There are those who have the authority to call and send ministers.

Authority to Minister

From the beginning of the Church, men have been set apart and given authority to lead and minister in the local church. For Anglicans, preparation for such ministry is governed by regulations (canons) and completed in a service found in the "Ordinal." Qualified and designated leadership is essential to congregational life and is necessary to avoid the chaos caused by competing authorities in one congregation. Since preaching and teaching are fundamental in Anglican worship, extensive study of Scripture and training in preaching are required standards for qualification to minister in the local congregation.

Authority to Ordain

For Anglicans, the authority to call and send ministers into local congregations is vested in the diocesan Bishop. In some Anglican provinces, vestries of local congregations have been given a voice in that process with the Bishop retaining the final approval.

The fact that this Article did not name the Bishop as the authority but uses the phrase "those who have the authority to call and send" is a sign of the ecumenical openness of the Articles. Other Churches of the Reformation did not have Bishops in historic succession, but that does not disqualify them as part of the one, catholic and apostolic Church. While Anglicans treasure the historic episcopate, they do not hold the view that where there is no Bishop there is no Church, as was taught by some in the early Church and is held by some Churches, even some Anglicans today. We need to be as ecumenical and open minded as our Articles urge us to be.

Prayer

Almighty God, by your divine providence you appointed various Orders of Ministry in your Church, and you inspired your Apostles to appoint those to serve therein. Behold those so called and fill them with the truth of your doctrine and adorn them with holiness of life, that by word, sacrament, and good example they may faithfully serve you to the glory of your Name and the edification of your Church, through the merits of our Savior Jesus Christ, who lives and reigns with you and the Holy Spirit, one God, forever and ever. *Amen.*

Scripture Texts

Acts 14:23 "And when they had appointed elders for them in every church, with prayer and fasting they committed them to the Lord in whom they had believed."

1 Timothy 3:1 "The saying is trustworthy: If anyone aspires to the office of overseer [this refers to both presbyters and bishops], he desires a noble task. Therefore, an overseer must be above reproach, the husband of one wife, sober minded, self-controlled, respectable, hospitable, able to teach, not a drunkard, not violent but gentle, not quarrelsome, not a lover of money."

Questions for Discussion

1. Have you ever been in a congregation that had weak leadership? What were the consequences?
2. What gifts in an ordained minister do you consider most important?
3. Is a layperson qualified to preach? To celebrate Holy Communion?

Article 24

Of Speaking in the Congregation in such a Tongue as the people understandeth

It is a thing plainly repugnant to the Word of God, and the custom of the Primitive Church to have public Prayer in the Church, or to minister the Sacraments, in a tongue not understood of the people.

The Reformation coincided with the translation of the Bible into "the language of the ploughboy," for which translators like William Tyndale gave their lives. The Reformers extended this principle of translation to worship: hence the Book of *Common Prayer*.

This Article makes two points: 1. churches are to conduct their worship in a language the people understand; and 2. failure to do so is contrary to Scripture.

Worship in the Common Language

The worship of God involves the whole person: mind, body, and will. This makes it mandatory that people understand what they are doing and the words they are hearing and saying. Given the prominent place of preaching the Word and celebrating the sacraments, a common language is even more essential. Where the people do not understand what is being said and done, they engage in private devotions or mere daydreaming in the service, which contradicts the purpose of gathering for common worship.

No Sacred or Special Language in Scripture

Although the Bible was written in Hebrew, Aramaic, and Greek, it contains no commands to make these languages sacred, and it has been now translated into thousands of local languages.

Well into the 20th century, the Roman Catholic Church conducted its worship in Latin on the grounds that Latin was a sacred tongue, and many of the Eastern Orthodox Churches sometimes use an ethnic language in worship in deference to the mother country. Not only does this turn away young people and lead to distractions mentioned above, but it has no basis in Scripture.

In accordance with this Article, Anglican missionaries have made translation of the Bible and the Prayer Book top priorities, and as a result Anglicans around the world worship in the languages of the countries and people where they find themselves.

Prayer

O God, our heavenly Father, you manifested your love by sending your only begotten Son into the world, that all might live through him: Pour out your Spirit on your Church that we may fulfill his command to preach the Gospel to all people. Through Jesus Christ our Lord and Savior. *Amen.*

Text

1 Corinthians 14:19 "Nevertheless, in Church I would rather speak five words with my mind in order to instruct others, than ten thousand words in a tongue."

Questions for Discussion

1. Have you ever attended a worship service conducted in a language that you did not understand? What was your reaction?
2. What do you think about using "thee's" and "thou's" in prayer and worship?
3. What are the positive benefits of worshiping in a language you and the congregation understand?

Article 25

Of the Sacraments

Sacraments ordained of Christ be not only badges or tokens of Christian men's profession, but rather they be certain sure witnesses, and effectual signs of grace, and God's good will towards us, by the which he doth work invisibly in us, and doth not only quicken, but also strengthen and confirm our Faith in him.

There are two Sacraments ordained of Christ our Lord in the Gospel, that is to say, Baptism, and the Supper of the Lord.

Those five commonly called Sacraments, that is to say, Confirmation, Penance, Orders, Matrimony, and Extreme Unction, are not to be counted for Sacraments of the Gospel, being such as have grown partly of the corrupt following of the Apostles, partly are states of life allowed in the Scriptures, but yet have not like nature of Sacraments with Baptism, and the Lord's Supper, for that they have not any visible sign or ceremony ordained of God.

The Sacraments were not ordained of Christ to be gazed upon, or to be carried about, but that we should duly use them. And in such only as worthily receive the same, they have a wholesome effect or operation: but they that receive them unworthily, purchase to themselves damnation, as Saint Paul saith.

This rather lengthy Article: 1. defines a sacrament in general; 2. defines the two sacraments of the Gospel; and 3. states the proper use of the Sacraments.

The Sacraments Defined

Sacraments are given us by God and are relational. He is the primary giver, and we respond in gratitude and surrender. It is important to consider of chief importance what it is that God is doing in the sacraments. For that reason, the Article begins by saying that the sacraments are far more than just what we are doing as expressions of our faith. Many Christians begin with *us* and never ask what *God* is doing. It is a weakness of those denominations that speak of Baptism and the Lord's Supper primarily or even exclusively as signs of our profession of faith. They are that, but so much more.

The Articles say the sacraments are "certain and sure witnesses," that is, they witness to us of God's grace, of His abundant, undeserved favor to us who have become His own in Christ. As we participate in the sacraments of the Gospel, God witnesses to us and speaks to us of His love for us.

The sacraments are "effectual signs of His grace and good will towards us, by which He works invisibly in us." God so relates to us in the sacraments that they effect something. "They are not bare signs," as Calvin put it, but are instruments by which God the Spirit works powerfully in our hearts, as we participate in humble faith.

Further, the Article states that God, in and through the sacraments of the Gospel, "quickens, strengthens, and confirms our faith in Him." Our trust in Him is awakened and deepened by His being graciously present to us and at work in us in the sacraments.

If Jesus' words – "wherever two or three are gathered together, there I am in the midst of them" – are encouraging, how much more do they apply when we are gathered to share in the sacraments of the Gospel that God through Christ has given us.

Two Sacraments of the Gospel

There are only two sacraments of the Gospel: Baptism and the Lord's Supper, also known as Holy Communion or Eucharist. They are called sacraments of the Gospel because they are centered in the heart of the Gospel, of Jesus' saving work for us. They alone were personally instituted by Christ, with a visible sign, a command and a promise attached. Being so central, the sacraments of the Gospel are offered to and enjoined on all Christians.

The Article goes on to mention five rites, practices, or states of life that have arisen in the Church's life that relate the love and truth of God to various moments and stations of our lives in Christ. They are not rightly called sacraments (Roman Catholic doctrine), for they lack the full marks mentioned above, but they are treasured and used one way or another in almost every Christian denomination.

Confirmation is an adult profession of faith before the congregation, important for all but especially for those baptized as infants. *Penance* is a special act of repentance and may or may not involve confession to a presbyter or fellow Christian. *Ordination* is the Church's recognition of God's call to the special ministry of Deacon, Presbyter (Priest) or Bishop. *Holy Matrimony* is the joining together of husband and wife in a lifelong, exclusive commitment to love, cherish, and serve one another by God's grace. This understanding of marriage is quite different from what our culture now means by marriage. *Extreme Unction* is the anointing with oil of those near death, and the practice is now extended to anointing for healing and other dedications.

The Proper Use of the Sacraments

This Article was written against several Roman Catholic practices which distort the purpose of the sacraments. We are told that we should duly use the sacraments, that is, we should celebrate them in a way appropriate to their purpose. For example, Jesus promised to be present in the elements of bread and wine when they were taken and eaten with thankful hearts in remembrance of His death. He did not command the elements to be carried about in procession, to be gazed at or venerated apart from the Eucharistic celebration itself.

Lastly, we are instructed to come in humble faith and in expectant gratitude to the Lord, Who is present to us in the sacraments. If we come and are just going through the motions, or for reasons of habit or to satisfy family or social pressure, they will not have a wholesome effect. The sacraments are effective only as part of our relationship with the Lord. In fact, we are warned by the Article and by Saint Paul that "anyone who eats and drinks without discerning the body eats and drinks judgment on himself" (1 Cor 11:29). May we all come to the sacraments with expectation and thanksgiving in our hearts.

Prayer

Almighty God, whose Son our Savior Jesus Christ is the light of the world: Grant that your people, illumined by your Word and Sacraments, may shine with the radiance of Christ's glory, that he may be known, worshiped, and obeyed to the ends of the earth; through Jesus Christ our Lord, who with you and the Holy Spirit lives and reigns, one God, now and fore ever. *Amen.*

Scripture Texts

Matthew 28:19-20 "Go therefore and make disciples of all nations, baptizing them in the name of the Father and of the Son and of the Holy Spirit, teaching them to observe all that I have commanded you. And behold, I am with you always, to the end of the age."

1 Corinthians 11:23-25 "For I received from the Lord what I also delivered to you, that the Lord Jesus on the night when he was betrayed took bread, and when he had given thanks, he broke it and said, 'This is my body which is for you. Do this in remembrance of me.' In the same way also he took the cup, after supper, saying, 'This cup is the new covenant in my blood. Do this as often as you drink it, in remembrance of me.'"

Questions for Discussion

1. What does the word "sacrament" bring to your mind?
2. Have you ever considered what God is doing in the sacraments?
3. If the sacraments are instituted to be effective in your heart and life, what sort of preparation might you take before coming to share in them?

Article 26

Of the Unworthiness of the Ministers, which hinders not the effect of the Sacraments

Although in the visible Church the evil be ever mingled with the good, and sometimes the evil have chief authority in the Ministration of the Word and Sacraments, yet forasmuch as they do not the same in their own name, but in Christ's, and do minister by his commission and authority, we may use their Ministry, both in hearing the Word of God, and in receiving the Sacraments. Neither is the effect of Christ's ordinance taken away by their wickedness, nor the grace of God's gifts diminished from such as by faith, and rightly, do receive the Sacraments ministered unto them; which be effectual, because of Christ's institution and promise, although they be ministered by evil men.

Nevertheless, it appertaineth to the discipline of the Church, that inquiry be made of evil Ministers, and that they be accused by those that have knowledge of their offences; and finally, being found guilty, by just judgment be deposed.

The Article opens by noting Jesus' teaching that in any church there will be a mixture of good and evil, of saints and sinners, and that some clergy will be living immoral lives, publicly or secretly, that bring scandal upon the church and the Gospel and that require church discipline. Blatant evil in a congregation is like yeast; it spreads. How much more does that happen if the evil is rooted in the leadership of the congregation.

This rather lengthy Article makes two simple points: 1. immoral ministers do not invalidate the Word and sacraments; and 2. immoral ministers should be charged and, if guilty, deposed.

Immoral Ministers and the Word and Sacraments

If one is aware that the ordained minister who is preaching the Word and administering the sacraments is morally compromised in a serious way, one might ask: "Can I gain any benefit from his preaching, even if it is biblical, or from the sacraments, even if he is using the Church's liturgy?" The answer is "Yes!" The efficacy of the Word and sacraments is not based on the worthiness of the ordained minister but on the gift and promise of God in Christ. And His grace is supplied by the Holy Spirit to all who participate in a faithful manner, no matter the spiritual state of the minister.

Discipline of Immoral Ministers

The fact that morally corrupt, hypocritical clergy cannot invalidate the efficacy of the Word and sacraments is no reason to ignore holding such clergy accountable. Church discipline in such cases is critical to the health of the Church. It is also a delicate matter. Jesus' teaching in this regard is a good rule of thumb for encountering evil-doers: start small and if necessary, "take it to the church" (Matt 18:15-18). Anglicans have ecclesiastical courts designed to get to the truth and to inform the Bishop whether the clergyman in question should be suspended from ministry for a time of repentance, renewal, and rebuilding of trust, or removed from the ministry altogether.

Prayer

Almighty God, whose blessed Son was led by the Spirit to be tempted by Satan: Come quickly to help us who are assaulted by many temptations, and, as you know the weaknesses of each of us, let each one find you mighty to save; through Jesus Christ your Son our Lord, who lives and reigns with you and the Holy Spirit, one God, now and forever. *Amen.*

Scripture Texts

2 Corinthians 4:5-7 "For what we proclaim is not ourselves, but Jesus Christ as Lord, with ourselves as your servants for Jesus' sake. For God, who said, 'Let light shine out of darkness,' has shone in our hearts to give the light of the knowledge of the glory of God in the face of Jesus Christ. But we have this treasure in jars of clay, to show that the surpassing power belongs to God and not to us."

1 Timothy 5:19-20 "Do not admit a charge against an elder except on the evidence of two or three witnesses. As for those who persist in sin, rebuke them in the presence of all, so that the rest may stand in fear."

Questions for Discussion

1. Have you ever been a member of a congregation led by a morally corrupt clergyman? If so, what was the effect he had on the congregation?

2. Would you have difficulty in receiving the Holy Communion from the hands of a corrupt clergyman? Why or why not?
3. What steps should you take to address the immorality of a clergyman whom you believe to be involved in sin?

Article 27

Of Baptism

> Baptism is not only a sign of profession, and mark of difference, whereby Christian men are discerned from others that be not christened, but it is also a sign of Regeneration or New-Birth, whereby, as by an instrument, they that receive Baptism rightly are grafted into the Church; the promises of the forgiveness of sin, and of our adoption to be the sons of God by the Holy Ghost, are visibly signed and sealed, Faith is confirmed, and Grace increased by virtue of prayer unto God.
>
> The Baptism of young Children is in any wise to be retained in the Church, as most agreeable with the institution of Christ.

This Article sets forth three points: 1. baptism is the sign of regeneration by the Holy Spirit; 2. by baptism people are signed and sealed and grafted into the Church, in which faith is confirmed and grace increased; and 3. the baptism of young children is to be retained as agreeable to Christ's institution.

Baptism a Sign of Regeneration

As is said in Article 25 and again in Article 28, while the sacraments involve our heart-felt participation, they are so much more than something *we do*. The chief actor in the sacraments is always God. After all, we are baptized at God's command into the name of the Triune God, Father, Son, and Holy Spirit.

We are saved by grace through faith, due to the work of the Holy Spirit regenerating our fallen hearts. Baptism is the visible sign of that regeneration. Baptism does not cause or ensure regeneration, but it is a promissory sign of regeneration and salvation through faith in Christ. In the case of babies, where baptism precedes genuine adult faith, the sign remains "effectual" as a promissory note, somewhat like a check which is cashed later.

Grafted into the Visible Church

The Church is the family of God on earth and in heaven. To be engrafted into the family of God is to be adopted as His child, and God becomes our Father. Also, the Church is the family of the forgiven and of those continually being forgiven, for we never completely stop sinning. Life in the Body of Christ is an intimate and daily refreshed relationship with the Triune God and with one's fellow Christians. Baptism is therefore a sign and seal (an assurance) of forgiveness freely given to His adopted children.

We should say a word about the meaning of "visibly signed." As we discussed with regard to the "visible church," baptism is the external sign of an invisible grace. We treasure the fact that God took the initiative and made us His own in and through our Baptism. Baptism is a public, visible act, visible to each other as fellow Christians. All the blessings that come to us through Baptism, they have as well, so we should treat one another as brothers and sisters in the family of God. Lastly, one's Baptism may become visible to those who hate Christians, and that is a cost we are asked to bear in some cultures.

To be baptized one must undergo instruction in the Faith. In addition, one must be ready and willing to make a series of promises that involve public participation in worship. When it is clear that the one seeking Baptism is ready to make those promises, the pastor administers baptism by immersion or pouring or sprinkling, thereby grafting that person into the visible Church, the community or body of Christ.

As noted in Article 25, the sacraments are "effectual" signs. Our faith is confirmed. In tough moments of pain or doubt, we may say, along with Martin Luther, "I am baptized! God has made me his own!" Through prayer to God, grace is increased and our faith strengthened as we turn to Him in prayer.

Infant Baptism

Although some Anglicans choose to defer baptism of their children, the Anglican Church has never agreed with those who only have place for believers' baptism. The attitude of Jesus to children, the baptism of whole households, and the example of circumcision of children in the Old Testament (cf. Col. 2:11) all point to retaining the baptism of infants and young children born and raised by Christians. Such baptism has in view the child's growing up into a personal faith in Christ, which Anglicans celebrate in the rite of Confirmation. In Confirmation a young person makes a public commitment to follow Christ. Any Church which retains infant baptism is called to take the nurture of its younger members and finally the preparation for Confirmation with great seriousness.

Prayer

We thank you, Father, for the water of Baptism. In it we are buried with Christ in his death. By it we share in his Resurrection. Through it we are assured we are regenerate by the Holy Spirit. Therefore, in joyful obedience to your Son, we bring into his fellowship those who come to him in faith, baptizing them in the Name of the Father, and of the Son, and of the Holy Spirit. *Amen.*

Scripture Texts

Mark 10:12-13 "And they were bringing children to him that he might touch them, and the disciples rebuked them. But when Jesus saw it, he was indignant and said to them, "Let the children come to me; do not hinder them, for to such belongs the kingdom of God."

Acts 2:38 "And Peter said to them, 'Repent and be baptized every one of you in the Name of Jesus Christ for the forgiveness of your sins and you will receive the gift of the Holy Spirit.'"

Acts 16:14-15 "One who heard us was a woman named Lydia, from the city of Thyatira, a seller of purple goods, who was a worshipper of God. The Lord opened her heart to pay attention to what was said by Paul. And after she was baptized, and her household as well, she urged us, saying, 'If you have judged me to be faithful to the Lord, come to my house and stay.' And, she prevailed upon us."

Questions for Discussion

1. Sacraments are rich in symbolic meaning. Our baptism has more meaning than most of us are aware of. Reflect on all that is symbolized as stated in the Article and how it applies to you.
2. The baptism of infants is still controversial. How would you defend it to a friend who is a Baptist?

Article 28

Of the Lord's Supper

The Supper of the Lord is not only a sign of the love that Christians ought to have among themselves one to another, but rather it is a Sacrament of our Redemption by Christ's death: insomuch that to such as rightly, worthily, and with faith, receive the same, the Bread which we break is a partaking of the Body of Christ; and likewise the Cup of Blessing is a partaking of the Blood of Christ.

Transubstantiation (or the change of the substance of Bread and Wine) in the Supper of the Lord, cannot be proved by Holy Writ; but is repugnant to the plain words of Scripture, overthroweth the nature of a Sacrament, and hath given occasion to many superstitions.

The Body of Christ is given, taken, and eaten, in the Supper, only after an heavenly and spiritual manner. And the mean whereby the Body of Christ is received and eaten in the Supper, is Faith.

The Sacrament of the Lord's Supper was not by Christ's ordinance reserved, carried about, lifted up, or worshipped.

The second Gospel sacrament is called "The Lord's Supper" in this Article. It is also known by various Anglicans as Holy Communion, the Eucharist, and the Mass (which, when it uses the Prayer Book, is not the same as the Roman Mass). It is not the name that matters but the significance of this sacrament.

This Article has four main points: 1. the Lord's Supper is a sacrament of our redemption; 2. the doctrine of transubstantiation overthrows the nature of a sacrament; 3. the Body of Christ is given and received in the Supper spiritually; 4. the sacrament of the Lord's Supper can be misused ceremonially.

A Sacrament of Redemption

At the center of the Lord's Supper is the reenactment of the Lord's institution of the sacrament at the Last Supper, in which Jesus was pointing to and interpreting the meaning of the Cross as God's great action in Christ for our redemption. His words "This is my Body" and "This is my Blood" make the sacrament something more than a mere memorial or mnemonic device but a real "participation" in Him (1 Cor 10:16). His command to "do this in remembrance of me" places the celebration of the sacrament of the Lord's Supper at the center of our worship and common life as Christians. At the heart of things, we are a redeemed people, bought and paid for by the blood of Christ. Everything else flows from that grace-filled reality.

As Christ has loved us and given us this sacrament of His righteousness and love revealed on the Cross, so ought we to love God and one another. In this deep sense the Lord's Supper is a "love feast," but is much more than that. Through the grace of the sacrament God enables us to love one another: "We love because He first loved us" (1 John 4:19).

The Error of Transubstantiation

The Roman Catholic Church teaches that the sacramental signs of bread and wine are physically changed into the actual body and blood of Christ. Thomas Aquinas explained that the visible appearance of the elements still looked like bread and wine after the substance had been changed because it would be hard for us to accept eating flesh and drinking blood, and because it gives us something to believe without seeing.

Anglicans object to this doctrine for several reasons. First, there are no grounds for this doctrine in Scripture. Jesus was clearly speaking symbolically when He instituted the Lord's Supper. Second, this doctrine overthrows the nature of a sacrament by confusing the visible sign with the spiritual reality that it visibly represents. Third, it has led to numerous abuses of the sacrament outside the context of the Lord's Supper itself.

The Body and Blood of Christ Received Spiritually

The sacraments are relational, from heart to heart. Jesus tells us that it is not what goes into our stomachs but what comes from our fallen hearts that defile us (Mark 7:18-19). Likewise, the grace of God in the sacrament of the Lord's Supper is not what enters the stomach but what is received spiritually in our hearts by faith. Anglicans are content to let the nature of the sacramental union of the bread and wine with the presence of Christ in the sacrament remain mysterious to our minds but real in our experience.

Misuses of the Sacrament

At the time of the Reformation, certain practices using the consecrated elements had grown up in the life of the Church, such as lifting the consecrated bread high during the Mass, displaying it in a procession, or reserving the consecrated bread and wine in a tabernacle on the Holy Table for private devotion. All these practices were abuses of the sacramental action of the Holy Communion service.

The frequent celebration of the Holy Communion is a great blessing, and it calls for us to participate in the sacrament in accordance with Christ's instruction and with humility, thanksgiving, and expectancy.

Prayer

Almighty Father, whose most dear Son, on the night before he suffered, instituted the Sacrament of his Body and Blood: Mercifully grant that we may receive it in thankful remembrance of Jesus Christ our Savior, who in these holy mysteries gives us a pledge of eternal life; and who lives and reigns with you and the Holy Spirit, one God, for ever and ever. *Amen.*

Scripture Texts

Matthew 26:26-28 "Now as they were eating, Jesus took bread, and after blessing it broke it and gave it to his disciples, and said 'Take, eat: This is my body.' And he took a cup, and when he had given thanks, he gave it to them saying, 'Drink of it, all of you, for this is my blood of the covenant which is poured out for many for the forgiveness of sins.'"

1 Corinthians 11:29 "For anyone who eats and drinks without discerning the body eats and drinks judgment on himself."

Questions for Discussion

1. Explain how partaking of the Holy Communion deepens your love for your fellow participants.
2. What do you consider the focus of the Lord's Supper to be?
3. What is the doctrine of transubstantiation? Why do Anglicans believe it is incorrect? And how has it led to abuses of the sacrament?
4. Why are we warned not to take the Holy Communion unless we are believing and repentant?

Article 29

Of the Wicked, which eat not the Body of Christ in the use of the Lord's Supper

The Wicked, and such as be void of a lively faith, although they do carnally and visibly press with their teeth (as Saint Augustine saith) the Sacrament of the Body and Blood of Christ; yet in no wise are they partakers of Christ: but rather, to their condemnation, do eat and drink the sign or Sacrament of so great a thing.

While all have sinned and fallen short of the glory of God, Christian and non-Christian alike, God offers through the sacrament forgiveness of sin to all those who heartily repent and turn to Him. This Article is addressed to the "wicked," which includes unrepentant believers and unbelievers who receive the sacrament "unworthily."

This Article has two points: 1. unrepentant Christians and unbelievers do not receive the body and blood of Christ when partaking of the Lord's Supper; but 2. by taking the sacrament unworthily, these people bring condemnation on themselves.

The Sacrament Voided

A sacrament is an outward and visible sign of an inner spiritual grace. The connection of the outer sign and inner grace is mysterious and remains undefined by Anglicans. The sacraments of the Gospel are personal, relational, and effective only when entered with repentant faith in Christ. Since the sacrament is addressed to the heart and not the stomach, when the heart is closed through sin or unbelief, there is only a partaking of the visible sign (consecrated bread and wine) but not the reality to which it points. In this respect, Anglicans are more like the Reformed Churches and at odds with both the Roman Catholic and Lutheran Churches, which claim that the "real presence" of Christ in the elements is inseparable from the visible sign. Not all Anglicans agree with this Article on this matter, but the Article is clear in what it says.

Condemnation for Unworthy Reception

To participate in the Lord's Supper in a casual, unbelieving manner is an expression of a deeper rejection of God and the Gospel. Those who do so not only fail to receive the benefits of the sacrament, but they bring down God's judgment on themselves. Such a practice has a bad ending in view and the New Testament urges us all to examine ourselves before we partake of the Holy Communion, lest we eat and drink damnation on ourselves.

Prayer

Gracious Father, whose blessed Son Jesus Christ came down from heaven to be the true bread which gives life to the world: Evermore give us this bread, that he may live in us and we in him; who lives and reigns with you and the Holy Spirit, one God, now and forever. *Amen.*

Scripture Text

1 Corinthians 11: 27-30 "Whoever, therefore, eats the bread or drinks the cup of the Lord in an unworthy manner will be guilty of profaning the body and blood of the Lord. Let a person

examine himself, then, and so eat of the bread and drink of the cup. For anyone who eats and drinks without discerning the body eats and drinks judgment on himself. That is why many of you are weak and ill, and some have died."

Questions for Discussion

1. How is it possible to receive the elements but not the blessing of the Lord's Supper?
2. How should one prepare oneself to participate in the Lord's Supper "worthily"?

Article 30

Of both Kinds

> The Cup of the Lord is not to be denied to the Lay-people: for both the parts of the Lord's Sacrament, by Christ's ordinance and commandment, ought to be ministered to all Christian men alike.

This Article makes one point: no Church has the right to deviate from Christ's institution of the sacrament and His command to "Do this in remembrance of me."

When this Article was being written, the Roman Catholic Church was offering only the consecrated host (bread) to the members of the Church. Although this practice grew up in the Church's life for practical reasons, it contradicts Jesus' plain words of institution. With joy we can now say that Rome has repented of that practice and distributes both the consecrated bread and wine to the laity.

The norm in Anglican Churches historically has been to offer wine in a common cup. For specific reasons, e.g., a viral pandemic, participants may dip (intinct) the bread in the wine, or receive it separately, remembering that one loaf and one cup represent the one Body of Christ.

Prayer

Almighty Father, whose most dear Son, on the night before he suffered, instituted the Sacrament of his Body and Blood: mercifully grant that we may receive it in thankful remembrance of Jesus Christ our Savior, who in these holy mysteries gives us a pledge of eternal life; and who lives and reigns with you and the Holy Spirit, one God, forever and ever. *Amen.*

Scripture Texts

Matthew 26:27 "And he took the cup, and when he had given thanks, he gave it to them, saying, 'Drink of it, all of you.'"

1 Corinthians 10:16 "The cup of blessing that we bless, is it not a participation in the blood of Christ? The bread that we break, is it not a participation in the body of Christ?"

Questions for Discussion

1. How has the recent coronavirus pandemic or other epidemics affected your practice of receiving Communion?
2. What is your opinion of replacing wine with grape juice?

Article 31

Of the one Oblation of Christ finished upon the Cross

The Offering of Christ once made is that perfect redemption, propitiation, and satisfaction, for all the sins of the whole world, both original and actual; and there is none other satisfaction for sin, but that alone. Wherefore the sacrifices of Masses, in the which it was commonly said, that the Priest did offer Christ for the quick and the dead, to have remission of pain or guilt, were blasphemous fables, and dangerous deceits.

This Article makes two points: 1. Christ's offering on the Cross is once for all and sufficient to cover the sins of the whole world; and 2. the continual "sacrifices" of Christ offered in the Masses of the Roman Catholic Church are unbiblical and a delusion.

The Sufficiency of Christ's Once-for-All Sacrifice

In His perfect sacrifice on the Cross as our representative and substitute, Christ made complete redemption (reconciling man with God at a ransom price), propitiation (satisfying the judicial wrath of God on sinners), and satisfaction (settling the debt we owe God, by taking our death and condemnation). Christ having done this once for all, there is neither need nor possibility of any other so-called sacrifices of Christ for merit (see Article 2).

The Delusion of Masses for Merit

One of the errors of Roman Catholic teaching was the idea that by offering Christ bloodlessly afresh at the communion altar, one accumulated merit in a kind of savings account. As a result, private altars and masses grew in large numbers. Donations could be given so that the merit would be applied to a chosen person for an earlier release from the suffering of purgatory.

In short, the doctrine and practice of the sacrifices of the Masses represent a profound error that leads the faithful away from simple trust in Christ and the sufficiency of His work upon the Cross. Anglicans took and continue to take the stand that it ought to be stopped as unbiblical and spiritually harmful.

Prayer

Assist us mercifully with your grace, Lord God of our salvation, that we may enter with joy upon the meditation of those mighty acts by which you have promised us life and immortality; through Jesus Christ our Lord, who lives and reigns with you and the Holy Spirit, one God, for ever and ever. *Amen.*

Scripture Texts

Hebrews 9:26-28 "Nor was it to offer himself repeatedly, as the high priest enters the holy places every year with blood not his own, for then he would have had to suffer repeatedly since the foundation of the world. But as it is, he has appeared once for all at the end of the ages to put away sin by the sacrifice of himself. And just as it is appointed for man to die once, and after that comes judgment, so Christ, having been offered once to bear the sins of many, will appear a second time, not to deal with sin but to save those who are eagerly waiting for him."

1 John 2:2 "He is the propitiation for our sins and not for ours only, but also for the sins of the whole world."

Questions for Discussion

1. How would you describe the fulness of Christ's work on the Cross?
2. In the Lord's Supper, what do Anglicans mean when "we offer ourselves, our souls and bodies to be a reasonable, holy, and living sacrifice"?

Article 32

Of the Marriage of Priests

> Bishops, Priests, and Deacons, are not commanded by God's Law, either to vow the estate of single life, or to abstain from marriage: therefore it is lawful for them, as for all other Christian men, to marry at their own discretion, as they shall judge the same to serve better to godliness.

This Article makes two points: 1. Scripture does not require the ordained clergy to be single; and 2. it is right for the ordained clergy to marry as God leads.

Celibacy Not Required by Scripture

The Roman Catholic Church requires Priests and Bishops to be single. Deacons may marry but only before they are ordained. In the Eastern Orthodox Church, Bishops must be single, and priests and deacons married before ordination may remain married after ordination. The Protestant Reformers broke with these requirements.

The practice of requiring the clergy to take a vow of celibacy is a requirement nowhere mandated in Scripture. The Apostle Paul points out that the other apostles had wives. Jesus mentioned that some men had the gift or vocation of celibacy, but that it is a gift to be personally and voluntarily embraced, not a requirement of the Church. To require men to remain single for life when they do not have the gift of celibacy has led to a great deal of sexual misbehavior and scandal in the Church down to this day.

The Choice to Marry or Remain Single

Ordained clergy should have the same right to marry as any other Christian. They also have the choice to remain celibate, so long as they are abstinent. Since the Reformation, Anglican clergy have never been refused the right to marry, although there have been prominent examples of Anglican clergy like John Stott who have chosen to remain celibate. This choice is affirmed in Scripture. Anglicans do have monastic communities in which the vow of celibacy is taken, but the choice to enter such communities is voluntary.

Prayer

O God, the giver of all that is true and lovely and gracious: We thank you for binding us together in these holy mysteries of the Body and Blood of your Son Jesus Christ, uniting us with him, and giving us a foretaste of the great marriage supper of the Lamb. Grant that by your Holy Spirit all those who come to be joined in Holy Matrimony, may become one in heart and soul, live in fidelity and peace, and obtain those eternal joys prepared for all who love you, for the sake of Jesus Christ our Lord. *Amen.*

Scripture Texts

1 Corinthians 7: 2 "But because of the temptation to sexual immorality, each man should have his own wife and each woman her own husband."

1 Corinthians 9: 5 "Do we not have the right to take along a believing wife, as do other apostles and brothers of the Lord and Cephas?"

Questions for Discussion

1. In 1 Corinthians, chapter 7, St. Paul states that he wishes all were as he is, unmarried. Why do you think he says this?
2. What are the advantages for a congregation of having married clergy in leadership and pastoral counseling?

Article 33

Of excommunicate Persons, how they are to be avoided

That person which by open denunciation of the Church is rightly cut off from the unity of the Church, and excommunicated, ought to be taken of the whole multitude of the faithful, as an Heathen and Publican, until he be openly reconciled by penance, and received into the Church by a Judge that hath authority thereunto.

This Article sets forth three points: 1. the Church has the authority and duty to excommunicate those persons found guilty of blasphemy; 2. excommunication must be carried out by the proper authority; and 3. the whole Church must honor the judgment on those excommunicated.

The Authority to Excommunicate

The word "excommunicate" is used in two ways. It can refer to a momentary ban from receiving the Lord's Supper while still attending worship. In this case, it may be done discreetly, without all in the congregation knowing. More seriously, excommunication can also refer to someone being publicly banned from the congregation altogether. Both acts of excommunication are done in the hope of repentance and restoration of those being excommunicated. This Article is referring to the second and severe form of excommunication.

When a member of the congregation, clergy or lay, unrepentantly and openly violates the doctrine or morals of the Church, the Church has both the authority and the duty to address the issue and to expel the person or persons until they have genuinely repented. This duty arises from the fact that sin like yeast tends to expand and permeate through the congregation. People begin to reckon that if it is being done openly and is not being condemned by the authorities, then it must be permissible and then even desirable. Excommunication is done both to protect the congregation and in hope for the one being excommunicated.

Excommunication by Proper Authority

Excommunication is so serious that it should only be done as the last option and by the proper authority. Jesus tells us that in cases of offenses in the church, one should go first to the offender alone, one on one, then with several others, and finally "take it to the Church." In the Anglican Church today, there are courts to examine evidence and finally, the bishop of the diocese, with consultation with his authorized Council, makes the declaration of excommunication. The person excommunicated is not to be involved in the worship or any of the regular activities of the congregation, or of any other congregation of the Diocese until ready to repent publicly and be formally reinstated.

Honoring the Judgment of Excommunication

Since the whole congregation is involved in the proper process of excommunication, the whole congregation is called to honor that decision. In the case of clergy or staff member, the decision will be announced, usually through a circular letter. If the excommunication is to have effect, the congregation must not undermine its severity, for the hope is that the loss of community will help open the eyes and heart of the person out in the cold, so to speak, and bring them to repentance.

When the person is repentant and restored by the Bishop, the congregation needs to welcome and warmly embrace the brother or sister so reinstated. The danger is that some will be like the elder brother and not welcome the prodigal home. For some kinds of offense, restoration to fellowship does not include return to leadership.

Prayer

Almighty and everlasting God, you hate nothing that you have made, and you forgive the sins of all who are penitent: Create and make in us new and contrite hearts, that we, worthily lamenting our sins and acknowledging our wretchedness, may obtain of you, the God of all mercy, perfect remission and forgiveness; through Jesus Christ our Lord, who lives and reigns with you and the Holy Spirit, one God, for ever and ever. *Amen.*

Scripture Texts

1 Timothy 5:20 "As for those who persist in sin, rebuke them in the presence of all, so that the rest may stand in fear."

2 Thessalonians 3:13-14 "As for you, brothers, do not grow weary in doing good. If anyone does not obey what we say in this letter, take note of that person and have nothing to do with him, that he may be ashamed."

Questions for Discussion

1. Have you ever heard from the pulpit a declaration of excommunication of a member of your congregation, or a friend in the local diocese? How did you react? What did you do and why?

2. What are the steps to excommunication in your Diocese or Church?
3. Why is it important that this all be done with the knowledge of the whole congregation?
4. What is the cause of the "Elder Brother" syndrome? How do we avoid it?

Article 34

Of the Traditions of the Church

> It is not necessary that Traditions and Ceremonies be in all places one, or utterly like; for at all times they have been divers, and may be changed according to the diversity of countries, times, and men's manners, so that nothing be ordained against God's Word. Whosoever, through his private judgment, willingly and purposely, doth openly break the Traditions and Ceremonies of the Church, which be not repugnant to the Word of God, and be ordained and approved by common authority, ought to be rebuked openly, (that others may fear to do the like,) as he that offendeth against the common order of the Church, and hurteth the authority of the Magistrate, and woundeth the consciences of the weak brethren.
>
> Every particular or national Church hath authority to ordain, change, and abolish, Ceremonies or Rites of the Church ordained only by man's authority, so that all things be done to edifying.

It may be helpful to understand this Article if we clarify several terms. First, "traditions and ceremonies" may extend from "catholic" summaries of the Faith such as the Nicene Creed to lesser practices like placing a Cross or candles on the communion table or singing hymns. Some "Puritans" in the 16th century objected to any tradition or ceremony that was not explicitly mentioned in Scripture. On the other hand, Roman Catholic and Orthodox Churches elevate Tradition to equal authority with Scripture. Article 34 expresses the Anglican "middle way," whereby, having determined that a tradition or ceremony is "congruent" with and not "contrary" Scripture, the Church then insists clergy and people conform to its standards of worship and governance (Prayer Book and canons).

This Article has three major points. 1. the traditions and ceremonies of the Church may vary from place to place and time to time so long as they are congruent with God's Word; 2. the stated traditions and ceremonies of a particular church are to be observed by individual members; and 3. national Churches have the right to add, change, or abolish those rites and ceremonies added by man as is helpful to the people.

The Variety of Traditions and Ceremonies

Changes in history, culture, and society will at times lead national Churches and even local congregations to make changes in their customs and practices. Therefore, all things will not be the same in every congregation throughout the global Church, or even within a given diocese. As the Prayer Book put it, such diversity is allowable so long as "the Faith be kept entire" and as long as the changes are harmonious with the Holy Scriptures, as read in the light of Christ. This is particularly relevant for Anglicans today in a global Communion of many tribes, languages, and nations.

Anglicans affirm the great value of tradition and tend to embrace as much tradition from the early Church on as is in harmony with Scripture, even beyond what is explicitly required by Scripture. However, in this view there will be, at times, the need to alter or even abolish some traditional practices when they no longer are helpful to the Church's growth in holiness or to fruitful mission.

Conforming to Traditions and Ceremonies

Most contemporary Churches allow for various choices in liturgy and music, and in outward ceremonies. However, the diversity within or between Churches is not to be taken as permission for an individualistic free-for-all. Some Christians may wish that their congregation did things in a particular way, but that does not give them the right to do their own thing. Clergy or laypeople who do take these matters into their own hands are accountable and ultimately subject to church discipline, lest others follow their example.

The Right of National Churches

The Articles were written for the established Church of England as the national church, and even today certain changes must be approved by Parliament. Elsewhere in the Anglican Communion, churches in those nations are not established, and it would be more accurate to speak of them as "denominational" Churches. Non-established churches have constitutions and canons which allow for changes, including Prayer Book revision.

A word of caution is in order. Since patterns of worship and polity are deeply rooted in the hearts and minds of the people, churches should be very careful in making sudden and radical changes.

Prayer

O God of unchangeable power and eternal light: Look favorably on your whole Church, that wonderful and sacred mystery; by the effectual working of your providence; carry out in tranquility the plan of salvation; let the whole world see and know things which were cast down are being raised up, and things which had grown old are being made new, and that all things are being brought to their perfection by him through whom all things were made, your Son Jesus Christ our Lord; who lives with you in the unity of the Holy Spirit, one God, for ever and ever. *Amen.*

Scripture Texts

Romans 14:19 "So then let us pursue what makes for peace and for mutual upbuilding."

Romans 16:17 "I appeal to you, brothers, to watch out for those who cause divisions and create obstacles contrary to the doctrine that you have been taught; avoid them."

Questions for Discussion

1. List some of the differences you have noticed as you have attended congregations other than your own. Did you find any that you wished your congregation would adopt? What did you do about that?
2. What are some of the things that must not vary from place to place in your judgment? Why?
3. Discuss a major change that your congregation or denomination has gone through. Could it have been handled better?

Article 35

Of the Homilies

The Second Book of Homilies, the several titles whereof we have joined under this Article, doth contain a godly and wholesome Doctrine, and necessary for these times, as doth the former Book of Homilies, which were set forth in the time of Edward the Sixth; and therefore we judge them to be read in Churches by the Ministers, diligently and distinctly, that they may he understanded of the people.

Of the Names of the Homilies.

1. Of the right Use of the Church.
2. Against Peril of Idolatry.
3. Of repairing and keeping clean of Churches.
4. Of good Works: first of Fasting.
5. Against Gluttony and Drunkenness.
6. Against Excess of Apparel.
7. Of Prayer.
8. Of the Place and Time of Prayer.
9. That Common Prayers and Sacraments ought to be ministered in a known tongue.
10. Of the reverend Estimation of God's Word.
11. Of Alms-doing.
12. Of the Nativity of Christ.
13. Of the Passion of Christ.
14. Of the Resurrection of Christ.
15. Of the worthy receiving of the Sacrament of the Body and Blood of Christ.
16. Of the Gifts of the Holy Ghost.

17. For the Rogation-days.
18. Of the State of Matrimony.
19. Of Repentance.
20. Against Idleness.
21. Against Rebellion.

From the American Book of Common Prayer (1801)

[*This Article is received in this Church, so far as it declares the Books of Homilies to be an explication of Christian doctrine, and instructive in piety and morals. But all references to the constitution and laws of England are considered as inapplicable to the circumstances of this Church; which also suspends the order for the reading of said Homilies in churches, until a revision of them may be conveniently made, for the clearing of them, as well from obsolete words and phrases, as from the local references.*]

If we take the original Article along with the American addendum, we end up with two points: 1. the Homilies are excellent in doctrine and morals and are included in the 39 Articles; and 2. the Homilies, as written, are not to be read today in local congregations as part of corporate worship.

The Virtues of the Homilies

The Homilies, which are model sermons, were provided by the Reformers as examples of biblical and orthodox teaching for use in congregations that had no clergy or whose clergy had little or no training in theology. As part of the 39 Articles, the Homilies embody its teaching and share in its authority.

The Limitations of the Homilies

The original Homilies had to do with their specific references to the Established Church of England. Two centuries later there is the additional problem of style. The Homilies are archaic, lengthy, with some obscure references, and obsolete words and phrases. We await a version of the Homilies that is something of a digest of each homily, expressed in a more readable and accessible style. In that case, they would be an excellent resource in Christian education and for private reading and study.

Prayer

Almighty God, you give your servants special gifts to understand and teach the truth revealed in Christ Jesus: Grant that by this teaching we may know you, the one true God, and Jesus Christ whom you have sent; who lives and reigns with you and the Holy Spirit, one God, for ever and ever. *Amen.*

Scripture Text

2 Timothy 2:2 "And what you have heard from me in the presence of many witnesses entrust to faithful men who will be able to teach others also."

Questions for Discussion

1. See if you can buy or borrow a copy of the Homilies and read two or three of them. You can probably find them online as well. Do you see the virtues of their substance and the difficulty of their use in current churches?

Article 36

Of Consecration of Bishops and Ministers

The Book of Consecration of Archbishops and Bishops, and Ordering of Priests and Deacons, lately set forth in the time of Edward the Sixth, and confirmed at the same time by authority of Parliament, doth contain all things necessary to such Consecration and Ordering: neither hath it any thing, that of itself is superstitious and ungodly. And therefore whosoever are consecrated or ordered according to the Rites of that Book, since the second year of the forenamed King Edward unto this time, or hereafter shall be consecrated or ordered according to the same Rites; we decree all such to be rightly, orderly, and lawfully consecrated and ordered.

From the American Book of Common Prayer (1801)

The Book of Consecration of Bishops, and Ordering of Priests and Deacons, as set forth by the General Convention of this Church in 1792, doth contain all things necessary to such Consecration and Ordering; neither hath it any thing that, of itself, is superstitious and ungodly. And, therefore, whosoever are consecrated or ordered according to said Form, we decree all such to be rightly, orderly, and lawfully consecrated and ordered.

The differences between the original Article and the American revision are superficial, again having to do with the difference of the Episcopal Church in America with the Established Church of England, but they do not touch the substance of the teaching of the Article.

This Article makes two points: 1. the Ordinal as used by the Anglican Churches and found in the Book of Common Prayer is fully adequate and in accord with the practice found in the Scriptures; and 2. those that have been ordained using this Rite are truly and lawfully ordained.

The Adequacy of the Ordinal

Ordination in the New Testament has three elements: the call, presence and prayers of the congregation and the laying on of hands by the Apostles and later the presbyter-bishops. When the Anglican Reformers were drawing up the liturgy for the Ordinal, they made certain that all three elements were present. In short, the ordinal is "full" in that nothing is left out that the Scriptures ask for and it is Scriptural in that it simply follows the example found in Scripture.

This Article arose in response to the charge by the Roman Catholic Church that Anglican orders were invalid because the rite did not adequately distinguish between priests (presbyters) and bishops and because the rite did not charge the priest to offer the sacrifice of the Mass. Anglicans replied that biblically, presbyters and bishops were not clearly distinguished, although the 1662 Ordinal later stated that "it is evident unto all men diligently reading holy Scripture and ancient Authors, that from the Apostles' time there have been these Orders of Ministers in Christ's Church; Bishops, Priests, and Deacons."

Anglicans did not include the so called "sacrifice of the Mass" because they considered it contrary to Scripture and dishonoring to the full and sufficient sacrifice of Christ on the Cross.

The statement that there was nothing superstitious in our rites is probably a response to some Puritans who raised a question about assuming that the Holy Spirit could be given by human laying on of hands and prayer. The response to that is that, as with other rites of the Church, God does use ordination effectively when rightly based on the example of Scripture and entered into in humble faith.

Legitimacy of Clergy

It should not be unsettling that Rome does not recognize Anglican orders, or that some other Protestants object to episcopacy or to holy orders altogether. Anglicans have remained faithful to Scripture and to the historic practice of the early Church. Those ordained as Anglicans are lawfully and truly ordained in God's one, true and holy catholic Church, and need never subject themselves to any act of reordination.

Prayer

Lord Jesus, you are the Good Shepherd who cares for his flock: We ask you to bestow upon your Church the gifts of the Holy Spirit in abundance, and to raise up from among us faithful and able persons called to the ministries of Deacon, Priest, and Bishop. Inspire them to spend and be spent for the sake of the Gospel and make them holy and loving servants and shepherds of the flock for whom you shed your most precious blood. Grant this for the sake of your love. *Amen.*

Scripture Texts

Acts 14:23 "And when they had appointed elders for them in every church with prayer and fasting, they committed them to the Lord in whom they had believed."

1 Timothy 5:17 "Let the elders who rule well be considered worthy of double honor, especially those who labor in preaching and teaching."

Questions for Discussion

1. Why is it inappropriate for a person ordained or consecrated in the Anglican Church to submit to reordination?
2. What is wrong with the idea of a priest "offering the sacrifice of the Mass" from the Anglican point of view?

Part Five

Christianity and Civic Responsibilities (Articles 37-39)

These Articles address several aspects of a Christian's relation to the State, and of the relation of Church and society. Due to the passage of six centuries and the unique Establishment of the Church in England, many of these Articles have been revised. However, basic principles of church and state remain important.

Article 37

Of the Power of the Civil Magistrates

The King's Majesty hath the chief power in this Realm of England, and other his Dominions, unto whom the chief Government of all Estates of this Realm, whether they be Ecclesiastical or Civil, in all causes doth appertain, and is not, nor ought to be, subject to any foreign Jurisdiction. Where we attribute to the King's Majesty the chief government, by which Titles we understand the minds of some slanderous folks to be offended; we give not our Princes the ministering either of God's Word, or of the Sacraments, the which thing the Injunctions also lately set forth by Elizabeth our Queen do most plainly testify; but that only prerogative, which we see to have been given always to all godly Princes in holy Scriptures by God himself; that is, that they should rule all estates and degrees committed to their charge by God, whether they be Ecclesiastical or Temporal, and restrain with the civil sword the stubborn and evil-doers.

The Bishop of Rome hath no jurisdiction in this Realm of England.

The Laws of the Realm may punish Christian men with death, for heinous and grievous offences.

It is lawful for Christian men, at the commandment of the Magistrate, to wear weapons, and serve in the wars.

From the American Book of Common Prayer (1801)

The Power of the Civil Magistrate extendeth to all men, as well Clergy as Laity, in all things temporal; but hath no authority in things purely spiritual. And we hold it to be

> the duty of all men who are professors of the Gospel, to pay respectful obedience to the Civil Authority, regularly and legitimately constituted.

As with Articles 35 and 36, the shorter American version was made due to the regime change after the American Revolution. America was no longer under a King, and the Episcopal Church was no longer an Established national church, which fact soon led to a plurality of Christian churches and denominations. Even in England after the 17th century, the King's role was balanced by the role of Parliament.

This version of Article 37 makes two main points: 1. the clergy as well as all citizens are subject to the civil authorities; and 2. civil magistrates have authority over temporal matters but have no authority over the spiritual matters of the Church.

This revision should not obscure the fact that the American Article agrees with the original Articles in terms of biblical teaching concerning church-state relations and the obligations of Christians as individual citizens of the state.

The longer version has four main points: 1. the King has the chief power in the realm of England and all its estates; 2. the King is not given jurisdiction over the ministry of the Word of God or of the sacraments of the Gospel; 3. the King through the magistrates has the power to restrain and punish evil-doers and, if the crime be heinous, to employ the death penalty; and 4. it is lawful for Christians to bear arms and to serve in the military in peacetime and in wartime.

The King's Chief Power in England

The Article was aimed in part at past claims by the Pope that clergy were under his rule and not subjects under British law. This claim is rejected. There is no scriptural basis for such a papal claim. God in His providence establishes nations and boundaries and puts people in positions of authority. The Roman Church has no temporal civic authority, much less international civic authority.

The Limits of the King's Power in Spiritual Matters

While the King may be called "head" or "supreme governor" of the Church of England, this title does not give him authority over the ministry of Word and sacraments or over the spiritual life and mission of the Church. The Church of England is an established Church, which gives some advantages to its life, ministry, and mission, but it is Scripture, not the King, that determines the Church's faith and morals. This principle of autonomy led eventually in England to the acceptance of "free churches" that upheld biblical principles and also to synodical governance within the Church of England.

The Power to Punish

As taught in Scripture, the State through its judicial courts and police instruments has the duty to keep order, protect the people and punish evil. If the crime is particularly heinous, as in intentional murder or treason, the State has the right to impose the death penalty.

Christians' Right to Bear Arms

Down through the Church's history, some have interpreted Jesus' call to love our enemies as a call to pacifism, and this view has been held by some "peace churches" to this day. This view, according to this Article, makes a category error in seeing individual ethics as identical with social ethics. Such an interpretation is contrary to many scriptural examples and to the mainstream of Christian social ethics, as taught, for example, by St. Augustine. Christians may with good conscience bear arms and serve as police and in the military, so long as they are not commanded to render obedience to the state over obedience to God.

Since the advent of denominationalism, governments in England and America have allowed for conscientious objectors to offer non-violent service in wartime and peacetime.

Prayer

Almighty God, our heavenly Father, send down on those who hold public office the spirit of wisdom, charity and justice; that with steadfast purpose they may faithfully serve in their offices to promote the well-being of all people; through Jesus Christ our Lord. *Amen.*

Scripture Texts

Psalm 144:1-2 *Of David*. "Blessed be the LORD, my rock, who trains my hands for war, and my fingers for battle; [2] he is my steadfast love and my fortress, my stronghold and my deliverer, my shield and he in whom I take refuge, who subdues peoples under me."

Luke 20:21-25 "So they asked him, 'Teacher, we know that you speak and teach rightly, and show no partiality, but truly teach the way of God. Is it lawful for us to give tribute to Caesar, or not?' But he perceived their craftiness, and said to them, 'Show me a denarius. Whose likeness and inscription does it have?' They said, 'Caesar's.' He said to them, 'Then render to Caesar the things that are Caesar's, and to God the things that are God's.'"

Matthew 26:52 "Then Jesus said to [his disciple in Gethsemane], 'Put your sword back into its place. For all who take the sword will perish by the sword.'"

Romans 13:1-3 "Let every person be subject to the governing authorities. For there is no authority except from God, and those that exist have been instituted by God. Therefore, whoever resists the authorities resists what God has appointed, and those who resist will incur judgment. For rulers are not a terror to good conduct, but to bad."

Questions for Discussion

1. Can you identify examples in our day of the Government stepping over the line and meddling in the spiritual ministry of the Church?
2. When is it right for Christians to disobey the Government?
3. What is your view of the death penalty?

Article 38

Of Christian Men's Goods, which are not common

The Riches and Goods of Christians are not common, as touching the right, title, and possession of the same; as certain Anabaptists do falsely boast. Notwithstanding, every man ought, of such things as he possesseth, liberally to give alms to the poor, according to his ability.

This Article makes two points: 1. Christians may possess private property; and 2. all persons should give liberally to the poor.

Christians and Private Property

Some early Anabaptists interpreted the practice of voluntary sharing in the earliest church in Jerusalem (Acts 2:44-45) as a precedent and mandate for all Christians to hold all things in common. The Articles rejected this precedent as a form of new legalism. While Christians are free to form communities, monastic or otherwise, into which people may enter voluntarily, there is nothing in Scripture that suggests that such a way of life is normative or required of all Christians. The Bible more generally assumes that people possess private property and are responsible to God for how they use it. We are stewards of all our "talents," material and otherwise, for it all belongs to God.

The Mandate to Care for the Poor

The Lord "loves a cheerful giver." Throughout the Scriptures God's people are enjoined to give liberally to the poor, the elderly, the disabled, and refugees (sojourners). This mandate presupposes that where work is available, people in good health will work. The Bible also recognizes the responsibility of the rich to help the poor, widows and orphans, and refugees from persecution ("sojourners"). The same principle applies to us today; though governments have developed many social welfare programs that seek to help the poor; even so, it is often Christians and churches that reach out to the poor more effectively.

Prayer

Increase, O God, the spirit of neighborliness among us, that in peril we may uphold one another, in suffering tend to one another, and in homelessness, loneliness, or exile befriend one another. Grant us brave and enduring hearts that we may strengthen one another, until the disciplines and testing of these days are ended, and you again give peace in our time; through Jesus Christ our Lord. *Amen.*

Scripture Texts

Deuteronomy 24:19 "When you reap your harvest in your field and forget a sheaf in the field, you shall not go back to get it. It shall be for the sojourner, the fatherless, and the widow, that the LORD your God may bless you in all the work of your hands."

Luke 6:20 "And he lifted up his eyes on his disciples, and said: 'Blessed are you who are poor, for yours is the kingdom of God.'"

2 Thessalonians 3:12 "Now such persons we command and encourage in the Lord Jesus Christ to do their work quietly and to earn their own living."

Questions for Discussion

1. What is the difference between a voluntary sharing of wealth out of a common love for God and each other and modern-day Communism and Socialism?
2. Why do you think the Scriptures put such a strong stress on supporting the poor?
3. Do you consider yourself answerable to God for how you use your wealth?

Article 39

Of a Christian Man's Oath

> As we confess that vain and rash Swearing is forbidden Christian men by our Lord Jesus Christ, and James his Apostle, so we judge, that Christian Religion doth not prohibit, but that a man may swear when the Magistrate requireth, in a cause of faith and charity, so it be done according to the Prophet's teaching in justice, judgment, and truth.

This final Article sets forth two main points: 1. casual and angry ("rash") oath-taking is forbidden to Christians; and 2. Christians may take an oath required by the State if it serves justice and is truthful.

Casual and Angry Oath-Taking Forbidden

Throughout history, men have taken oaths in the name of their god or gods. Christians are not to take the Lord's Name in vain. Your name is precious to you. People have been known to take their own lives because they have in some way besmirched their name. In biblical times a person's name was very significant, telling a great deal about his or her character, ambitions, and reputation. How much more so God. In the Ten Commandments God tells us not to use His Name in an empty fashion or in false testimony. His Name brings Him into the picture and conversation.

Nor is it permissible for us to use the Lord's Name in anger, that is, loudly or repeatedly without thinking. In God's eyes, idle cursing and swearing is as offensive as perjury in court. Some people have so developed their patterns of expression so that the Lord's Name is mentioned in almost every sentence. No Christian is permitted to do this, no matter how hard it is to break such a habit. We are to keep in mind that God will not hold any of us as guiltless who abuse His Name. The New Testament expands on the negative commandment by urging us to swear not at all and speak the truth in love (Eph 4:15; James 5:12).

Legitimate Oath-Taking

Some Anabaptist Christians interpreted Jesus' teaching in the Sermon on the Mount to "let your yes be yes" to forbid oaths altogether. This view is extreme. In the Letters in the New Testament, we find the Apostle Paul and others, from time to time, confirming their teaching or actions by making a solemn vow. God Himself, when making the covenants, takes oaths in His own Name (Deut 32:40).

As was the case in the previous two Articles, Anglicans make a distinction between an individual's personal manner of speech and those solemn times when the State requires an oath. Anglicans have concluded that on such governmental occasions, it is acceptable to the State to require and for a Christian to agree to swear an oath "so help me God." Of course, any such oath must be in the cause of justice and our testimony must be fully truthful.

Prayer

Almighty God, your truth endures from age to age: Direct in our time, we pray, those who speak where many listen and write what many read; that they may speak your truth to make the heart of this people wise, its mind discerning, and its will righteous; to the honor of Jesus Christ our Lord. *Amen.*

Scripture Texts

Leviticus 19:12 "You shall not swear by my Name falsely, and so profane the Name of the Lord your God: I am the Lord."

Mark 14:70-71 "And after a little while the bystanders again said to Peter, 'Certainly you are one of them, for you are a Galilean.' But he began to invoke a curse on himself and to swear, 'I do not know this man of whom you speak.'"

2 Corinthians 1:23 "But I call God to witness against me, it was to spare you that I refrained from coming again to Corinth."

Questions for Discussion

1. What in your opinion is the difference between vain and rash swearing? Why are both forbidden us as Christians?
2. Have you ever been asked to take an oath in court or on an official document? Did that pose a problem for you? Why or why not?